A B
OF CHRIS

O God, you are my God;
eagerly I seek you;
my soul thirsts for you,
my flesh faints for you,
as in a barren and dry land
where there is no water.

Psalm 63:1 (LBW)

This book is for Linda.

A BRIEF HISTORY
of
CHRISTIAN
SPIRITUALITY

BRADLEY P. HOLT

AUGSBURG COLLEGE

A LION BOOK

Copyright © 1993, 1997 Bradley P. Holt
First published in the USA by Augsburg Fortress

The author asserts the moral right
to be identified as the author of this work

Published by
Lion Publishing plc
Sandy Lane West, Oxford, England
ISBN 0 7459 3721 7
Albatross Books Pty Ltd
PO Box 320, Sutherland, NSW 2232, Australia
ISBN 0 7324 1585 3

This edition first published 1997
10 9 8 7 6 5 4 3 2 1 0

A catalogue record for this book is available
from the British Library

Printed and bound in Great Britain
by Cox and Wyman Ltd, Reading

CONTENTS

Preface

This book is intended for seekers. It is for people who have not yet seriously studied Christian spirituality. You the reader may be a person who wants to explore the meaning of Christianity for personal experience. You may be a church member whose congregation has not taken an interest in spirituality. You may be a person questing for wholeness and wonder what Christians have to offer. Or you may simply be curious about the interest in spirituality and how it relates to Christianity.

This book was written both for the interested individual and for the classroom, whether it is in college, seminary or church. I wrote it because there was no appropriate text for my courses in Christian Spirituality at Augsburg College. I looked in vain for a brief treatment of the Christian tradition which incorporated the features of this book: simplicity, global perspective and practical application. Though I do not feel that my knowledge or experience make me worthy to write a book with such a wide scope, the need for such an introduction overcame my hesitation and I was able to write about Christian spirituality as shaped by my deep convictions.

My own interest in spirituality became explicit while I was in graduate school at Yale University in the late 1960s. I had tried to find a way to write my dissertation within the field of systematic theology, but wound up writing on the history of spirituality instead. My dear friend and mentor, Dr Bernhard Christensen was finishing his book, *The Inward Pilgrimage*, at this time. Later, teaching at the Theological College of Northern Nigeria opened my eyes to the global scope of contemporary Christianity and the strength of African Christian spiritual life.

A short introduction like this one cannot attempt to discuss all the major figures in the tradition. The choices have been very difficult, but necessary for the scope of this book. Fuller treatments are noted in the bibliography, some of them excellent guides which contain extensive detail. For the sake of simplicity, endnotes have been kept to a minimum.

It has been my intention to use inclusive language in this account, but quotations from previous studies do not follow the standards of gender neutrality.

I want to thank a few of the many people who have helped in the years of preparing this manuscript. I thank the students in my classes for helpful comments and suggestions, Augsburg College for a sabbatical leave spent partly in South Africa, Namibia and the United Kingdom, the Hoversten Peace Grant, Harriet Lystig and Frances Holt for helping to finance that journey, and the librarians at the Augsburg Library and Luther Northwestern Seminary Library for helping me obtain materials. Special thanks to those who read the manuscript—Cynthia Englund, Darrell Jodock, Bradley Hanson, Eric Lund, John Ackerman, Ryan LaHurd, Ann Julian van Abel, Jon Fure, Carolyn Lystig, Lynne Lorenzen. I thank editors Irene Getz, Ron Klug and Maurice Lyon. Most of all, I thank the person who has most helped to shape the manuscript into user-friendly English, Linda Holt.

Spirituality and Christianity

Part of the human predicament is not always knowing what one really needs. Another part is the difficulty of acting consistently on what one does know. For example, I have had a problem listening to my body. I get tired or listless during the day and take a break to eat. Or I get upset or discouraged and eat. I smile at the refrigerator motto: 'If all else fails, eat!' For a long time I did not know that my body craved water, not food. I have discovered that just plain water will usually perk me up better at mid morning or late afternoon than the various combinations of caffeine, sugar and fat which settle on my front. I have come to recognize thirst as different from hunger, and to respond to my body's genuine need, at least some of the time!

One of the basic premises of any spirituality is that our non-physical selves also thirst. We may not know what we need, and we may try to satisfy our needs with possessions, foods, or relationships that do not satisfy and that may bring dangerous side effects. Christian spirituality identifies what we really long for as the living water of God, fresh and sparkling and pure. Long ago a woman from Samaria thirsted for this water.[1] She met Jesus, who saw her spiritual need and offered her living water. This water is not merely moving liquid, as she at first supposed, but is the Spirit of the living God.[2]

A second premise, crucial for Christians, is that God's love actively seeks the thirsty. It's as if wanderers in a dry land were trying to function in a state of dehydration. But the travellers do not recognize the thirst, or else they try to fulfil their need for water by eating salted peanuts or crisps! God in this parable approaches the wanderers in Jesus as a servant, a water-carrier and guide. He bears the water and points them to a beautiful fountain running over with the water of life.

Is 'Christian spirituality' an oxymoron?

For many people, the term 'Christian' and the term 'spirituality' do not fit together. Many see spirituality as an alternative to Christianity, for they contrast spirituality with religion, and they see Christianity as a religion. (This view would seem to exclude the possibility not only of Christian spirituality, but of Jewish, Muslim, Hindu, or Buddhist spirituality.) According to this view, religions have doctrines, creeds, buildings, clergy and budgets. Such institutions are interested in their own preservation and are not much interested in helping people with their problems. Some see the Christian tradition as so entrenched in patriarchal abuse or devaluing of women that it must be abandoned. Others see Christians as unwilling to accept those who struggle with addictions to alcohol or other drugs.

Such people are eager to learn about spirituality but not about Christianity. They are on a personal search for a meaningful relationship with the sacred, but are put off by the insistence on church attendance, the meagre instruction in technique, and the impersonal nature of much church life. Other traditions may seem to have a meaningful discipline, an ancient tradition and an openness to discovery. I ask you, seeking reader, to consider with an open mind whether Christianity has these very elements, when considered in its wholeness.

Many people have been wounded by the church, by its indifference, its gossip, its sexism or racism. As a member of the Christian community, the church, I want to ask your forgiveness, if you have experienced rejection from your church. Please reconsider the validity of the Christian walk, the Christian spiritualities described in this book. The treasure of the gospel of Jesus is contained in the truly earthen vessels of human followers. It is the message of that gospel and the Healer to whom it points which attracts people, in spite of the faults of local and national churches.

While some seekers for the spiritual may be put off by the churches, many Christians, especially pastors and theologians, may be put off by the teachings found in popular books on spirituality. It may seem to them that spirituality is nothing more than the latest fad in self-improvement. 'Spirituality' is a vague term which people use to include anything they want. For Protestants in particular, the term is unfamiliar; it's not part of the traditional language.

Furthermore, 'spirituality' looks suspicious to some Christians because it sounds like 'do-it-yourself' salvation. If you only do this or that, the books may suggest, you will find fulfilment or self-realization. This is very different from finding peace with God through repentance and faith in Christ.

So is it appropriate to speak of 'Christian spirituality'? Yes, it is. In fact the term 'spirituality' was first used among Christians. One need not be Christian to have a spirituality, but Christianity can be the basis for a vibrant and personal spirituality.

I believe the churches need to listen more to the groups and individuals who are seeking a spirituality, and that persons in various new age or self-help groups would do well to give Christianity a second chance. On the one hand, many churches have not responded to the longing of the human heart for a knowledge of God by experience, and not simply through books. The churches have generally done very little to help members or visitors grow in personal disciplines such as prayer and meditation or to understand the traditions concerning these central practices. Adults can be introduced to a variety of approaches, since not every person functions in the same way. At the same time, support groups are important for personal guidance. Thus churches need to encourage an individual exploration and experience of the faith, in the context of the church's practice of communal worship.

Individual seekers, on the other hand, would do well to become aware of the long history of spiritual practice in the church. Like the blind man who touched one part of the elephant, one person's experience is too limited to discover reality. Previous experience through the ages serves as a guide— both encouragement and warning. Furthermore, churches that live up to their calling offer an individual seeker the personal community that is essential for balanced Christian spirituality.

Any spirituality depends upon a view of reality for its validity. Some teachers of the spiritual may not be very open about their world-views. In the case of Christianity, that world-view is laid out in its theology, a simple version of which is found in the Apostles' Creed. A healthy spirituality will also be connected to ethics. Any spirituality whether it claims to be Christian or not, which does not include responsibility towards other people is self-defeating. Seeking a spiritual thrill or high without concern for the one who lacks food or clothing is spiritual malpractice. Christian spirituality includes more than an introspective search for psychological health; it integrates relationships to God and creation with those to self and others.

Christian spirituality is historical and global. It is an array of twenty centuries of development. It involves global connections with others whose cultures are very different from our own. I am convinced that in teaching about spirituality the churches do not sufficiently draw upon either the historic tradition or the sisters and brothers around the world. We need one another! For example, Henri Nouwen, one of the best known writers on spirituality in North America remarks,

> In the free world of the United States, where most of the world's wealth is concentrated, spiritual freedom is often hard to find. Many Christians in the North are imprisoned by their fears and guilt... The spiritual destiny of the people of North America is intimately connected with the spiritual destiny of the people in Latin America. I am increasingly struck by the thought that what is happening in the Christian communities of Latin America is part of God's way of calling us in the North to conversion.[3]

What Nouwen asserts here for North and South America is a specific example of what I am urging for all of us: that each of our continents has challenges—and gifts—for Christians elsewhere. We in the 'West' do have such challenges and gifts to offer, yet it may be true that North America and Western Europe are the most in need of help. Our churches are often lethargic compared with those of Africa, Asia and Latin America.

Our awareness is often as limited in time as it is in space. We think that the best resources must be found in the latest writer. Rather we need to look back through the centuries to learn from others of different times as well as different continents. We need to engage in a conversation with Christians of the past, whose mistakes as well as triumphs challenge our own assumptions and lifestyles.

What you can expect from this book

I am inviting you, the reader, to an inter-continental and inter-generational conversation about spirituality. This book is an attempt to survey the varieties of Christian spirituality both in space and time. From a late twentieth-century Western perspective, it looks back in time and around the continents to point out what is valuable for thirsty persons of our time. It tells the multicultural story of Christian history as it relates to spirituality.

After a preliminary discussion of the term spirituality and an overview of the Christian community on a global scale (in this chapter), the discussion will focus on the Bible, the essential literary source of Christian spirituality (in the second chapter). Then in succeeding chapters we explore the early centuries, the medieval age, the reformation, the 'modern' period, and the twentieth century. The last chapter will draw together themes and suggestions for the future.

Spiritual exercises which relate to the subjects of each chapter may be found in Appendix 2. Do try them out! Experiment with new ways of living. Each person has different needs in terms of practice. These suggestions may widen your range or deepen your experience.

The movements and individuals selected for this book reflect my vision of spirituality. More will be said about this later, but for now, let me indicate some criteria for choosing the subject matter which follows. I have included the most influential figures which any history of Christian spirituality must include, for example, Augustine, Teresa of Avila and John of the Cross. But I have also gone outside the usual 'canon' to include (a) Protestants and Orthodox as well as Catholics, (b) more women than is customary, and (c) non-Western Christians.

The spiritual tradition includes some well-known names, but it also includes the ways of countless ordinary folk whose names have been forgotten. What is commonly called 'popular piety' is also part of this story. The spirituality which is written in a 'spiritual classic' both reflects and influences common Christians. Some of this book will describe popular movements such as charismatic Christianity, pietism, or twelve-step spirituality. A great deal of it, however, will recount the stories and writings of the 'elite' who have influenced many others by the potency of their devotion and the power of the pen. Philip Sheldrake's *Spirituality and History* reminds us that interpreting the past is complex, and there are many pitfalls. One needs to have a critical eye for both the 'elite' whose books are remembered and for the interpreter of the texts, who sees value in them for the present.[4]

Sometimes I will include matters of general history or church history for background, even though these are not strictly matters of 'spirituality'. Many people find it helpful to be reminded about the events which shaped the story of spirituality. A time line is included in Appendix 1 for those of you who would like to consult it. I have also included a glossary of specialized terms, as well as indexes of names and subjects.

'Spirituality' for Christians means a style of walking in the Holy Spirit

'Spirituality'—this ambiguous, six syllable term is new to many and objectionable to some. Although it is a clumsy word, it is used so much because it seems to do a task that no other word does. 'Religion' for many people connotes an established system and institution, whereas 'spirituality' implies personal involvement. 'Spirituality' is a trans-religious word; it is not tied to one single faith. Thus one can speak of Hindu or Muslim spirituality, or even spirituality not rooted in a particular religion. In earlier centuries, many Christians used the words 'devotion' or 'piety'. But unfortunately these older terms have developed a flavour of other-worldly sentimentality. 'Spirituality' does not have this connotation, and is more clearly inclusive of daily life in the world.

'Spirituality' is easily misunderstood. It is commonly used, for example, to refer not to a type or style, but to a degree of 'spiritualness', so that it could be measured like a degree of temperature or humidity. This usage has the negative result that people tend to measure themselves or others as being more spiritual or less spiritual, and can even use the term as a club to batter others thought to be less 'spiritual' than they are themselves. I will avoid this way of using the term. I prefer to think of a spirituality, as a type or style of relating to God and the world.

From a Christian perspective, 'spirituality' calls us to recognize the importance of its root term, 'spirit', an important biblical word. In both Hebrew and Greek, the same word (*ruach* and *pneuma*, respectively) is used for breath, wind and spirit. The Bible refers both to human spirit and to divine Spirit. How one understands spirit will determine how one understands spirituality. For example, if 'spirit' is separated from physical reality, in a realm of its own, apart from the daily life of human experience, the resulting spirituality will become an escape into another world. But if God created the world good, and later became flesh, as the Gospel of John asserts, then 'spirit' is a dimension of reality, compatible with physical existence. Then humans are not divided, but rather, unities of body, mind, and spirit. The result is that spirituality has a much more holistic and down-to-earth meaning. It encompasses the whole of human life, and will develop in a variety of styles, depending on cultures, denominations, personalities, and gifts.

Catholic theology first used the term 'spirituality' in something like the present-day usage. For most of the centuries of the church theologians included the practice of Christianity in their discussions of doctrine. But in the eighteenth and nineteenth century 'mystical theology' and 'ascetical theology' became specialized fields. The first described the teachings of the mystics, the extraordinary Christians of the tradition; the other discussed the path of ordinary Christian disciplines. In the twentieth century these two subdisciplines combined into one: 'Spiritual theology' or 'Spirituality'. Various 'schools' of spirituality were recognized, which corresponded to the better known religious orders. Thus, Catholics began to write about Jesuit (or Ignatian) spirituality, Franciscan spirituality, Carmelite spirituality, etc. Eventually a spirituality for the laity was also discussed.

In the first half of the twentieth century Roman Catholic theologians assumed a number of ideas: that only Roman Catholics were genuine Christians; that there was unity among the varieties of Catholic spirituality; that spirituality grows out of the doctrines of theology; that the members of religious orders have a better track to perfection than the laity; and that the goal of all spirituality is the mystical vision of God. Because the Second Vatican Council (1962–65) produced a refreshing reassessment of Catholic faith, some of these assumptions have been questioned.

It is only in the past thirty years or so that Protestants have used the term spirituality, and the reasons for the delay are partly basic disagreements with the Catholic assumptions. But the ecumenical advance in the years since Vatican II has increased the conversation between the two traditions. Now there are studies describing the distinctive types of spirituality in the Protestant denominations, just as in the Catholic orders. Here are two recent descriptions of 'spirituality' from the *Dictionary of Christian Spirituality*:

> Prayer in Christian theology and experience is more than pleading or petition; it is our whole relation to God. And spirituality concerns the way in which prayer influences conduct, our behaviour and manner of life, our attitudes to other people. It is often best studied in biographies, but clearly it shapes dogmas, inspires movements and builds institutions.[5]

> SPIRITUALITY. This is a word which has come much into vogue to describe those attitudes, beliefs, practices which animate people's lives and help them to reach out towards super-sensible realities...

This means that Christian spirituality is not simply for 'the interior life' or the inward person, but as much for the body as for the soul, and is directed to the implementation of both the commandments of Christ, to love God and our neighbour. Indeed, our love, like God's, should extend to the whole of creation. Christian spirituality at its most authentic includes in its scope both humanity and nature.[6]

My own understanding of the term in the Christian context is that it refers in the first place to lived experience: 'If we live by the Spirit, let us also walk by the Spirit,' Paul writes.[7] The starting point is the Spirit of Christ living in the person, but the person is always considered in the context of a community, the body of Christ. Spirituality describes a particular *style* of Christian discipleship. For example, Jesuits or Lutherans or feminists each have a particular combination of themes and practices which make them distinctive. Note that each member of these groups has distinctive gifts and traits as well. Each group or person has its own flavour. This book will give you a small taste of many flavours.

In the second place, I understand 'spirituality' to refer to a theological field, an academic discipline, which might better be called 'spiritual theology' as opposed to 'doctrinal' or 'systematic' theology. This field attempts to describe and classify, to understand and evaluate, various types of Christian spirituality. It also creatively proposes ways for the Christian tradition to grow in the writer's own time and place. *A Brief History of Christian Spirituality* is an introductory example of such an enterprise.

What is the value of studying the global Christian tradition?

A living tradition is a self-critical developing stream, not a moribund repetition of the past. Tradition is the shoulder of previous experience on which we stand as we reach upward for what is new. Education involves studying the various traditions that have shaped a community, pondering the problems of continuity and change, and making decisions about adopting or rejecting elements of those traditions. Tradition is thus much wider than 'customs'; it includes narratives, doctrines, and values. 'Tradition is the living faith of the dead, traditionalism is the dead faith of the living.'[8]

Citizens of the United States, for example, have had to re-evaluate the impact of Christopher Columbus, the beliefs of the drafters of its founding documents, and the Vietnam War. Some elements of American tradition are very precious and deserve honour, but others, such as racism and greed, show that the nation needs repentance just as individuals do, and that new attitudes and practices are in order.

The Christian community lives as an inheritor of almost two millennia of thought, action, and prayer by people seeking to live in the power of the Holy Spirit. Great saints have exemplified the courage and love of Jesus, living witnesses of God's power to redeem. But the history of Christianity is also marked by continual departures from the way of its Lord, of social and personal injustice, error and violence. Therefore being heirs of a tradition does not mean approving everything in it. Rather, it means sifting out what is valuable from what is not, and creatively developing neglected strands of thought.

It is vitally important for Christian spirituality today that we take a wide view of that tradition and the global family of Christians, not simply repeating the small portion which may be familiar from our home, congregation, or ethnic group. The sweep of that tradition will open our eyes to wide resources of spirituality and give guidance for our own choices.

Perhaps no one has stated the need for reading books from the previous ages so pointedly as C.S. Lewis in his introduction to a fourth-century theological/spiritual work of the young Athanasius.

Every Age has its own outlook. It is specially good at seeing certain truths and specially liable to make certain mistakes. We all, therefore, need the books that will correct the characteristic mistakes of our own period. And that means the old books... Nothing strikes me more when I read the controversies of past ages than the fact that both sides were usually assuming without question a good deal which we should now absolutely deny... We may be sure that the characteristic blindness of the twentieth century—the blindness about which posterity will ask, 'But how *could* they have thought that?'—lies where we never suspected it... None of us can fully escape this blindness, but we shall certainly increase it, and weaken our guard against it, if we read only modern books... The only palliative is to keep the clean sea breeze of the centuries blowing through our minds, and this can be done only by reading old books. Not, of course, that there is any magic about the past. People were no cleverer then than they are now; they made as many mistakes as we. But not the *same* mistakes. They will not flatter us in the errors we are already committing; and their own error, being now open and palpable, will not endanger us. Two heads are better than one, not because either is infallible, but because they are unlikely to go wrong in the same direction.[9]

For perspective on the assumptions of the spirituality of our own age, assumptions which need to be questioned, nothing is better than reading the spiritual classics.

The first function of a study of the tradition and the present-day Christian family is to make us aware of our own narrowness, our own parochialism. Knowing a larger part of the whole tradition gives us better questions to ask of the fads of the present. We are endangered not only with ethnocentrism, judging all things by the customs of our own ethnic group, but also 'presentism', judging all previous ages as inferior to our own.

Secondly, the study of the tradition displays the variety of approaches to Christian spirituality. Too often we have thought that there is only one way of Christian prayer, or one way of following Jesus. The tradition shows over time a great cloud of witnesses, a treasure-house of approaches to living in discipleship to Jesus.

Varieties of approach include differences of emphasis on different biblical truths, such as we have in different denominations. Just as there are four Gospels, each bringing out different perspectives on the same Redeemer, so our denominations crystallize around different starting points within the story of the one Christ.

The varieties also include national cultural differences. Christianity began in a Jewish setting, very soon became Greco-Roman, Syrian, Armenian, Ethiopian and Celtic, and today is found in virtually every major cultural group in the world.

And of course the differences are personal. The Christian God is a respecter of the variety of personality, so that women and men of every type have followed the Way, and left markers for introverts and extroverts, people who mostly use their emotions and those who use their intellects to face the world. These can be seen for example in women as diverse as Teresa of Avila and Teresa of Calcutta; in men with different temperaments such as Francis of Assisi and Thomas Aquinas. What is the effect of studying this great variety of Christian spirituality, past and present? It is to widen the options available, to loosen my grip on non-essentials, it is to increase my wonder at the fellowship of which I am a part.

In its third function, the Christian tradition not only displays variety, but also presents norms or boundaries for that variety. Although there are many ways of living a spiritual life in the power of the gospel, there is only one Lord, one baptism, one God. The norms of genuine Christian spirituality are pre-eminently the Scriptures, but also the creeds of the early church. Theological norms are the statements of world-view, statements about the way things are, which form the skeleton on which the flesh of spirituality depends. For example, some people in early centuries thought that spirit was better than matter, and began to forbid eating or sex or bathing. It was the faith that God created the world good which helped to hold this dualistic spirituality in check.

Yet there are practical norms for spirituality, in addition to the theological ones. These determine how helpful a particular proposal will be in a given situation. A manner of shaping the Christian life may be perfectly orthodox doctrinally, but not meet the needs of people. This was common experience in colonial days in Africa, when European models were only partially helpful for new African Christians. Today Africans are seeking truly indigenous styles of spirituality which do not require them to become culturally European in order to become religiously Christian.

There is a very big playing-field for Christians, but there are also boundaries outside which the game is no longer Christian. In our day these lines are not always as clear as they seemed in past centuries, and many think that this is appropriate, to give space for exploration. Nevertheless, not every spirituality is a Christian spirituality, and that distinction is necessary for the identity and integrity of the tradition. My view is that Christians need to have their ears and hearts open to learn from other religious and cultural traditions, for example the Native traditions of North America, but not lose the centrality of Jesus Christ and the Bible as normative for their spirituality.

Christian history looks like an hourglass

Christianity is not a European religion, although today many people view it as such. The story of its expansion shows that Christianity can as truly be claimed as an Asian or an African religion as a European one. Jesus and his disciples were not Europeans, in spite of countless paintings which suggest that they were. Their culture was Middle Eastern Judaism, and their biological inheritance was from the ancient Hebrews, whose roots have no contact with Europe.

Perhaps we think of Jesus as European because American Jews today are mostly European, and we assume wrongly that he must have looked like them. In fact, Jews come in all colours, and it is not clear what color Jesus' skin might have been. Some say that he was likely to be short and dark-skinned. The point is that Jesus should not be seen as the founder of an ethnic faith for white-skinned Europeans, but as a universal figure whose message can rightly be claimed by all peoples. The artistic depiction of an African Jesus, a Chinese Jesus, or a Native American Jesus all express that conviction.

We may simplify Christian expansion to the peoples of the world into four main stages and picture it as an hourglass. The earliest and latest periods are 'wide' while the middle is 'narrow'.

First came a time of expansion from western Asia to three continents: eastward into Asia, southwest to Africa, and northwest to Europe. We read in the Acts of the Apostles in the New Testament that the gospel spread from Jerusalem to Judea, to Samaria, and to the ends of the world. The narrative introduces an African into the account (Acts 8) even before Paul travels to Europe with the good news (Acts 16). During this early period, there was no political or economic pressure for people to become Christians, but quite the opposite. The intrinsic merits of the faith were all that motivated acceptance of it.

Because of roads and trading routes, Christianity spread very rapidly in all directions. In the first century it probably reached Roman Britain as well as Egypt, Arabia and Armenia. Armenia was the first of the nations to declare itself Christian. It is claimed that the Mar Thoma Church in India and the Ethiopian Church also date from the first century, and we can be sure that they have their roots in this ancient period, even if the date accepted by Western historians is somewhat later.

So, if Christianity stretched from India and even China in the east to Britain in the west, from the Danube in the north to Ethiopia in the south, it is clear that at first Christianity was not just a Roman faith, nor even a European one, but truly a faith found in many cultures on three continents.

But a withdrawal marked the second period. After (1) the establishment of Christianity by Rome and Constantinople in the fourth century, (2) the doctrinal splits of the fifth century and (3) the rise of Islam in the seventh, the African and Asian churches were reduced to small minorities or completely disbanded.

The emperors after Constantine gradually moved from recognizing Christianity as a legal religion to making it the official state religion of the empire. This Byzantine connection between emperor and Christianity led to two unintended results. The rulers of other empires, Persia, for example, began to see the faith as the state religion of their enemies, and thus to persecute its followers as disloyal to their homelands. Secondly it meant that complaint against the church became a complaint against the state, and vice versa. Doctrinal disputes became political matters. Some of the peoples who were ruled from Constantinople became ripe for conversion to Islam because of their unhappiness with the rule of the distant emperors.

The Council of Chalcedon in 451 defined the teaching about the person of Christ, his divine and human natures, in a way that many Africans and Asians refused to accept. They were branded Monophysites or Nestorians, even though it is questionable that they differed fundamentally from the powerful churches related to Constantinople and Rome, who accepted the Chalcedonian definition. The definition stated that Jesus Christ is one person with two 'natures', human and divine. The Monophysites rejected the idea of two 'natures' and insisted that Jesus Christ had one divine-human nature.

Many Asian and African Christians who were alienated from the emperor in Constantinople by these doctrinal disputes welcomed the arrival of the Arabs in the seventh century, and eventually adopted Islam. They did so not at the point of the sword, but over time, under social, political, and economic pressure from the Muslim governments.

During this second period Christianity was gradually indigenized in Europe, where it continued to expand. For more than a thousand years, this faith dominated southern Europe; the northern peoples of Russia and Scandinavia were won over only after kings' decisions around AD1000. Christian theology and spirituality came to be shaped by Europe's various cultures—Greek, Roman, Celtic, Germanic, Slavic and Norse. For example the celebration of Christmas on 25 December and the use of a Christmas tree or yule log are adaptations of Christianity to previous European religions.

It came to be assumed that Christianity and European culture were one and the same; the universal character of Christianity was in danger of being lost. Some theologians even argued that since other peoples had not believed the gospel at Pentecost in the first century, it was useless to give them a second chance now, for God had obviously chosen the Europeans as his own and left the others out in the cold!

A new expansion from Europe to all the continents characterized the third period, from the sixteenth to the mid-twentieth century. First Roman Catholic and then Protestant missionaries took the message of the cross to all continents. Further, the vast emigration of Europeans to the Americas, Australasia, and South Africa made Christianity dominant in those areas. The political background of this expansion included European imperialism, first Portuguese and Spanish, then Dutch, English and French, and finally the economic and cultural dominance of the United States.

Christianity spread by emigration and by mission work from the North Atlantic, in a Europeanized form, often with little regard for the cultures and religions it replaced. There were just enough exceptions to this generalization to show that the Christian gospel was never entirely imprisoned by European political or cultural captivity. This period was fundamental to our present situation in providing both its possibility and its problems: the possibility of a world Christian community, not just a 'white man's religion', and the problems of a distorted gospel, which has suffered from European hegemony, racism, tribalism and sexism.

Today, in the fourth period of development, the spread of Christianity is not only from the Europeans. The churches of most countries are involved in evangelization domestically or internationally. The churches of Africa and Asia are also re-evaluating inherited forms of the gospel and discarding those aspects of European Christianity which are not fitting in their cultural setting. The churches of Latin America are struggling to overcome the economic imbalances rooted in the colonial period. Christianity is weakening in its old North Atlantic strongholds and growing in the continents of Africa, Latin America and Asia. This century, which was predicted to be the one in which all religions would die out, has proved on the contrary to be a time of rejuvenation for all the major world religions, including Christianity, in the non-Western world.

Thus one may view the story of Christianity as a sort of hourglass, with wide geographical extent in the early and most recent centuries, but a narrow stem of European isolation in the middle. It is obvious from this that a sound approach to the story of Christian spirituality must take into account movements and individuals outside of Europe. My aim here is to bring together two fields of knowledge which do not often connect: first, histories of Christian spirituality, which often concentrate on Europeans, and secondly scholarship concerning Western missions and new indigenous movements. The early non-Western spiritualities are as important to the study as the recent ones, and I will discuss them in Chapter 3.

As we look back on this story we see that Christianity has been crossing cultural boundaries from its start on the day of Pentecost, and up to the present. The translations of the Bible are a witness to this, with today's consciousness of 'contextualization' its climax. 'Contextualization' is the process in which Christianity speaks to a group of people in language and symbols with which they are at home, and they in turn express their Christian faith within their culture. The model for this process is seen to be the Word of God, who became fully human in Jesus of Nazareth, who was incarnated in human flesh, and in a particular history and culture.

This account was written in North America, but the basic idea applies everywhere. Christians in Europe, Latin America, Africa, Asia and Australia with the South Pacific, all will gain from sharing with one another. Such sharing is important not only between the industrialized and industrializing societies (the 'North' and the 'South') but especially among the industrializing societies ('South'–'South' relationships). And wisdom will come from studying not only the spirituality of the present but that of the past which informs our present.

More about the author's perspective

None of us is 'neutral' about matters that are important to us. Academic subjects which aim at objectivity are still coloured by the values of their researchers, professors, and sponsors. The fact that we each see things from our own perspective does not imply that the world of learning is hopelessly chaotic and 'subjective', but rather that we need to take into account the personal values and commitments of the speaker or writer, and then seek to learn, even if our own perspective is quite different. We take what is good and leave the rest.

As a way of introducing myself, I might list some important factors which have shaped my views of the world. I am a Protestant, a Lutheran who sees great value in the Orthodox and Catholic traditions, who sees Jesus Christ, the gospel, and the Bible as normative for interpreting the Christian spiritual traditions. My spouse Linda and our three children, Olaf, Karin and Paul have helped me to grow up, to accept myself, and to take responsibility.

I am a North American male of Scandinavian heritage who has been changed by nearly a decade of life in Africa, teaching at the Theological College of Northern Nigeria. I believe that the study of Christian spirituality needs to include non-Western sources, people of colour and women.

Having studied for many years in institutions of higher education, my approach to religion has been very intellectual, academic, 'left brain'. My interest in spirituality is due in part to the needs of the other side of my human nature, the experiential, emotional, spontaneous, 'right brain'. On one level, this book is an attempt to bring these two together.

Recommended Reading

Original Texts

The most comprehensive set of primary sources is found in the SPCK series *Classics of Western Spirituality*. The translations are recent, with introductory essays to set the context for these writings. The set will include more than fifty volumes when it is complete.

Comprehensive surveys

Cheslyn Jones, Geoffrey Wainwright and Edward Yarnold, editors, *The Study of Spirituality*, SPCK, 1994.
This is the single most helpful volume for reading further in the history of Christian spirituality. The thick paperback also includes sections on the theology of spirituality and on pastoral spirituality. There are extensive bibliographies on all of the figures discussed; it is a comprehensive reference written by many authors.

Bernard McGinn and John Meyendorff, editors, *Christian Spirituality: Origins to the Twelfth Century*; Jill Raitt, editor, *Christian Spirituality: High Middle Ages and Reformation*; Louis Dupre and Don E. Saliers, editors, *Christian Spirituality: Post Reformation and Modern*, 1987–89. (Volumes 16–18 of *World Spirituality*, SCM Press)
This three-volume collection of articles gives a comprehensive survey of the tradition.

Shorter surveys

Robin Maas and Gabriel O'Donnell, OP, editors, *Spiritual Traditions for the Contemporary Church*, Nashville: Abingdon, 1990.
Simon Tugwell, OP, *Ways of Imperfection*, Springfield, Illinois: Templegate, 1985.

Rowan Williams, *Wound of Knowledge: From the New Testament to St John of the Cross*, Darton, Longman and Todd, 1990.

These one volume surveys are very useful. The first includes exercises for the reader, while the second two have particular emphases on the cross and on living with imperfection.

A dictionary

Gordon S. Wakefield, editor, *Dictionary of Christian Spirituality*, SCM Press, 1990.

Short entries on most topics are included here. It is a very helpful reference.

About the 'hourglass'

Kenneth Scott Latourette, *A History of the Expansion of Christianity*, 7 volumes, London/New York: Harper Brothers, 1937–45.

This is an old classic describing in detail all of the ages up to World War II.

About the Christian tradition

Justo L. Gonzolez, *A History of Christian Thought*, 3 volumes, New York: Abingdon, 1970–75.

This is a very good survey of the tradition for beginners.

Jaroslav Pelikan, *The Christian Tradition: A History of the Development of Doctrine*, 5 volumes, Chicago: University of Chicago Press, 1971–89.

For advanced students of the tradition.

Academic study of spirituality

Bradley C. Hanson, editor, *Modern Christian Spirituality: Methodological and Historical Essays*, Atlanta: Scholars Press, 1990. (American Academy of Religion Studies in Religion, Number 62)

Philip Sheldrake, *Spirituality and History: Questions of Interpretation and Method*, New York: Crossroad, 1992.

Four Relationships in the Bible

The foundational documents of Christian spirituality are the Holy Scriptures. All later developments have their matrix in the divine–human dialogue recorded in the Bible. Though it has been interpreted in somewhat divergent ways, the canon of Scripture is recognized as the norm by all major Christian traditions. To set forth the teaching of the Bible on Christian spirituality would fill many books. The richness of its text is endless.

So, what this chapter will attempt is to select some of the biblical teachings on the four basic relationships which I believe constitute spirituality: our relationships to God, to self, to others and to creation. The selection of concepts and passages reflects my understanding of what is most important for these themes and what I see as having been neglected.

The discussion assumes a preliminary acquaintance with the Bible. If the Scriptures are unknown to you, reading a brief introduction to the Bible would be helpful. See the end of this chapter for suggestions.

The Bible is not simply one book but a whole library, written and collected over centuries by many writers in different situations. Thus it must be interpreted with care, not taking one verse as the 'answer' to a present-day problem, but looking for the main themes of the whole.

The Bible functions in a number of ways in its approach to spirituality. Firstly, it is food for spirituality. Much of the Bible is narrative, and the stories illumine the daily walk. Finding the connections between my story or my people's story and the biblical stories is the key to interpreting these ancient documents. Meditative reading of the Bible, listening to it preached or seeing it portrayed in a film, play, or painting, can feed the soul. The Bible portrays God, Jesus, the Holy Spirit in ways that convey good news to the reader or listener. The Bible becomes a living word from God when the Spirit speaks directly to our needs.

The Psalms have a special place in Christian spirituality as model prayers from all emotional levels. Their general character makes them appropriate for individuals with specific, contemporary problems. The Psalms are chanted by Catholic monks, included in the Book of Common Prayer by Anglicans, sung metrically by Presbyterians and the Church of Scotland, and used by members of all denominations in public worship and private devotion.

The Bible is also a norm or standard for the theology and ethics which interact so profoundly with spirituality. That is, the basic world-view and values of Christianity are taught and demonstrated in the Bible. They function as presuppositions for all Christian writing. For example, the Bible teaches that God created the world and declared it good. It teaches that God became human in Jesus and that his death and resurrection form the basis for human salvation. It teaches that God's love operates in our lives through the Holy Spirit, poured out at Pentecost.

The Bible calls us to welcome God's love in Christ and to love God

When Jesus is asked to name the greatest commandment he quotes Deuteronomy and then Leviticus.[1] The first is to love the Lord your God with all your heart, soul, mind and strength. Whatever else the Bible says about God which is relevant for spirituality, this is fundamental. God is to be loved with the whole self.

But who is this God? It is the God whose blazing love first created and then redeemed us. This God tenderly, jealously, sometimes wrathfully, sometimes joyously loved ancient Israel. This God took human flesh, was mocked and was killed to set free all peoples from sin, evil and death. The simplest description of this One is 'God is love'. Spirituality is welcoming this love into our lives; allowing it to change our habits, feelings, and thoughts; and thus returning the love to God who gave it.

Fundamental to any particular spirituality is its view of God, intellectually and emotionally. The intellectual side comes out in doctrines about God's nature. The emotional side comes out in prayers of celebration and mourning. Both sides are expressed in stories and metaphors, which abound in the Bible.

The Hebrew Bible or Old Testament gives us the basic understanding of God which dominates the whole tradition. The delicate balance of what can be known of God and what is beyond human understanding is expressed in a number of ways. God speaks to Moses, for example, 'face to face, as one speaks to a friend', but when Moses wants to see God's glory, he is told, 'you cannot see my face; for no one shall see me and live.'[2]

Isaiah likewise expresses a very definite claim to know the character of God, while reserving God's mystery:

> Have you not known? Have you not heard?
> The Lord is the everlasting God,
>   the Creator of the ends of the earth.
> He does not faint or grow weary;
>   his understanding is unsearchable.
> He gives power to the faint,
>   and strengthens the powerless.[3]

The relationship to God in prayer that is portrayed in the Bible also shares this tension between the known and the unknown. The Bible both teaches about prayer and illustrates it. God is One who can be addressed by humans and who addresses them. Prayers have great variety in the Bible, showing that there is no one form of address acceptable to the Almighty. Moses and Abraham see God as a friend and sometimes argue or barter with him. Job boldly accuses God. The Psalms contain bitter laments and joyful praises. Jesus prays for healings, gives thanks, submits to the Father's will, and calls out in forsakenness on the cross. Paul is lifted to the third heaven and cannot tell what he saw. In all of these we see God as the known and the unknown. This tension will later show itself in the history of spirituality as the *kataphatic* and *apophatic* approaches to God (see Chapter 3).

God in the Old Testament is known as the one who led the people out of slavery, who entered into covenants with individuals and the people of Israel, who revealed the Ten Commandments, who spoke through the prophets, and yet said,

> For as the heavens are higher than the earth,
>   so are my ways higher than your ways
>   and my thoughts than your thoughts.[4]

In so far as God is known, God is seen as creator of the world,[5] liberator of Israel,[6] judge of all people,[7] saviour of the faithful[8] and Holy One.[9] These universal metaphors are supplemented by a number of more personal ones. God is Friend, Father, Mother, Husband. Further, God is compared to non-personal parts of creation: God is mother bear, mother eagle, a lion, a rock, a fortress and fire. The images of God all fall short, yet are essential for human understanding. God is none of the things listed, God is not male or female. Yet God's personal, holy, living character is important for both Jews and Christians.

The New Testament builds on the Old Testament picture, but with a breathtaking assertion: God became incarnate in a human being! It is not that the Old Testament God is a God of wrath, while the New Testament shows a God of mercy, for both aspects of God can be seen in both Testaments. But the New Testament claims that the love of God for humanity was so great that God condescended to take human form in Jesus of Nazareth. This action affirms the goodness of creation as stated in Genesis 1, and affirms the value of human beings and human culture. For marred by evil as people may be, God entered the human story in a particular place and time.

Jesus himself describes God as a shepherd seeking one lost sheep, as a woman seeking a lost coin, as a father welcoming home a lost son. He addresses God as *Abba*, the Aramaic word for a father addressed by a small child. The closest we may have is 'Dad', or 'Daddy'. Thus Jesus lived out an intimate relation to God, modelling prayer and obedience to his own followers, but also inviting them to share in the oneness he experienced with the Father.

Paul, the apostle, writes that God declares sinners righteous, and through the Holy Spirit also indwells them, giving spiritual gifts and producing spiritual fruit. He brings us back to the issue of God's revelation and God's mystery. He is very confident of some truths, for example when he writes, 'For I am sure that neither death, nor life, nor angels, nor principalities, nor things present, nor things to come, nor powers, nor height nor depth, nor anything else in all creation, will be able to separate us from the love of God in Christ Jesus our Lord.'[10] But just a short while later, after writing about the will of God for Jews and Gentiles he concludes, 'O the depth of the riches and wisdom and knowledge of God! How unsearchable are his judgments and how inscrutable his ways!... For from him and through him and to him are all things. To him be glory for ever. Amen.'[11]

The Bible calls us to love ourselves

The second great commandment according to Jesus is to 'Love your neighbour as yourself.' The main point is love of neighbour, but implied is love of the self. Some recent writers have gone overboard in trying to correct a misleading teaching about the self by making this commandment say, 'look out for number one'. You cannot love your neighbour, they say, unless you love yourself first. So forget about your neighbour's needs until your own psychological problems are worked out. Give yourself all that your heart desires, and do not concern yourself with the poor. Such teaching goes directly against what it is meant to interpret.

Yet, Jesus did not say, 'love your neighbour and hate yourself'. A proper concern for the self is the standard of care for the neighbour here. A distinction must be made between love for oneself and selfishness. The former involves care, nurture, responsibility, faithfulness; the latter is greedy, exploitative, and idolatrous. To love oneself rightly is neither to grab from others to satisfy one's desires, nor to neglect the care which we all need physically, psychologically and spiritually.

The Bible does not define the self, but describes the relations people have with God, others and creation. Psalm 139 is a meditation on the wonders of God's relation to the self, in God's creative knowledge and ubiquity. Genesis describes the person in terms of a body with the breath of life from God. This breath is the same word as 'spirit'.

The Bible generally views a person as a unity of body, soul, mind, heart and spirit. It does not separate these elements the way some philosophers have tended to do. Thus the self in the Bible is the whole person, intellect, will, emotions, conscious and unconscious, social and private, whatever distinctions have been made. It is this whole self that is called upon to love God, serve and praise God.

The human being is seen in the Bible as someone made in the image and likeness of God as well as a fallen person, subject to sin and evil. The Bible describes human bondage and promises freedom. Thus the integration and healing of the self is implicit in the message of the Bible, in such explicit teachings as redemption, liberation, forgiveness and resurrection.

Throughout the Bible people are called to repent from evil. In the New Testament the most common word for repentance means turning around, changing direction. By God's grace, human beings are not only able to perceive some of what alienates them from God, but also to receive new life, new direction, new birth.

The Bible calls us to love other persons

When Jesus explained the second great commandment, he told the story of a Samaritan who helped a bleeding man on the road. The vision of Christian spirituality includes not only 'my God and I', but the world of need in which Christians have always lived. Not only care for the poor but standing up for those who are being treated unjustly is part of the Christian life.

Different kinds of love are called for in different situations. Love for refugees whom we have never seen except on television calls for practical aid, but no personal relationship. Among those we know, our community of faith, our family, and our friends are special types of relationships which call for more intimate kinds of love.

Christian spirituality has a special place for other persons who share the faith. It is not only personal but communal. The Bible does not know of separating individuals from the people of Israel or from the church; our relations with God are as members of a body, not as isolated individuals. It is as a people that we celebrate the Lord's Supper and share in Christ's body and blood. It is the community that is Christ's body, not an individual. The gifts of the Spirit are given to the community, not just individuals.

Families are important groups for spiritual nurture. The compassion and trust we show one another shape the lives of children for years to come. It is in the family that most of us learn to pray, to read the Bible devotionally, to forgive one another, to assume our responsibilities.

Spiritual friends are also important in Christian growth. Aside from the community in general, individual guides and companions can help us see ourselves in ways that we cannot on our own. It is only when someone else has seen our sins that assurance of God's forgiveness has power for us. The word of grace is heard more credibly from another than a self-absolution.

It is the field of Christian ethics that studies our relation to other persons most directly. The complex ethical problems facing Christians today force us to listen carefully to the specialists who remind us of the context and the specifics of the Christian tradition that undergird us in making concrete decisions. It is important not to separate ethics from spirituality, lest spirituality be a private escape from the real world, a self-fulfilment at the cost of others. Ethics and spirituality belong together.

The Bible calls us to love the creation

The two creation accounts in Genesis both affirm the goodness of the world and human existence.[12] The first account of seven days repeatedly proclaims 'That is good', whereas the second makes clear God's approval. They both urge care for the natural world. Modern society has distorted and disregarded our accountability, as we exploit the earth for only human interest. The basis for Christian understanding of the world is the assertion that creation is good, but is not God. The beauty and power of nature have led some to worship it; the Bible reminds us to worship the Creator, not the creature. The transience and cruelty of nature have caused some to despise and mistreat it; instead the Bible reminds us to be good caretakers or stewards.

Christian spirituality has not always given proper attention to the natural world. The influence of Neo-Platonism and other ancient philosophies has been to view the world as an uncomfortable and transient prison. The ambiguity of the word 'world' in the Bible has permitted this distortion. Especially in John, the term 'world' can be used for humanity organized against God, or as 1 John has it, 'all that is in the *world*, the lust of the flesh and the lust of the eyes and the pride of life, is not of the Father but is of the world'.[13] Obviously the writer is not talking about the same world which God loves in John 3:16: 'For God so loved the *world*, that he sent his only Son, that whoever believes in him should not perish but have eternal life.'

So the term 'world' has at least three meanings. It can refer to the created world which God called good in Genesis 1. Or it can refer to humanity, as in John 3:16. Finally it can refer to human evil, and it is this usage which has sometimes led to distortions in Christian spirituality. Both Catholic monks and Protestant Pietists have sought to love God and not love the world. But sometimes they have needed a St Francis or a C.S. Lewis to remind them of the goodness of the natural world and the joyful pang of its beauty.

Meanwhile, it is the duty of Christians today to care for the earth and to integrate this into their spirituality. Too long has it been a neglected aspect. As the Psalms praise God for the natural world (e.g. Psalm 104), and Jesus used natural parables ('look at the birds, look at the flowers...'), Christian appreciation for the work of God needs to be matched in our day by taking responsibility for lifestyle and economics in order to preserve the creation from human destruction.

We read in the Bible of a new heaven and a new earth, of a resurrection of the body and of the earth somehow giving birth to a redeemed creation.[14] These eschatological teachings are not properly a call to regard the earth with indifference, but to value it as God does, to prepare for the last day, whatever form the transformation takes, into a new existence in a renewed creation.

Recommended Reading

David and Pat Alexander (eds), The Lion Concise Bible Handbook, third edition, Oxford: Lion Publishing, 1996.

William Barclay, *Introducing the Bible*, Nashville: Abingdon, 1972.

Mary Batchelor, *Opening up the Bible*, Oxford: Lion Publishing, 1993.

George Carey (ed.), *The Bible for Everyday Life*, Oxford: Lion Publishing, 1988.

Charles Cummings, *Eco-Spirituality: Toward a Reverent Life*, New York: Paulist Press, 1993.

Walter Trobisch, 'Love Yourself', in *Complete Works of Walter Trobisch*, Downers Grove, Illinois: InterVarsity, 1987, pages 653–92.

The Beginnings of a Global Community

The first followers of Jesus were Jews, and Christianity became one sect, the 'Nazareans', among others. But the beliefs of this sect—which saw Jesus as the Promised One, not only Messiah, but suffering servant, crucified for all and raised from the dead—led it to be rejected by other Jews, especially after the destruction of the Jerusalem temple in the year AD70. Christians had largely escaped from Jerusalem, so did not share the suffering of other Jews; they also attributed the destruction to the rejection of the Messiah. This Jewish sect was then excluded from synagogue worship by a curse on Christians inserted into the synagogue liturgy.

Thereafter, Judaism and Christianity separated, siblings created in the first century from the common stock of the people of Israel. The Judaism of today is the offspring of the rabbinical movement which emerged fully about the same time as Christianity. Each group came to interpret the Hebrew Bible (the Old Testament) by means of a later collection of their own literature. The Jews used the Talmud, the Christians the New Testament.

The good news about Jesus came to be preached to Gentiles, especially those called 'God-fearers', who were attracted to local Jewish synagogues but did not choose to be circumcised in order to become Jews. Paul preached to such people in his travels, according to the Acts of the Apostles. Because of the Jewish rejection, the percentage of Jewish Christians dwindled, but the Gentiles gladly heard this message, which included the monotheism and high ethical standards of Judaism, without the requirement of circumcision.

What happened here was that Christianity emerged from being a sect within an ethnic group into a religion accessible to all peoples. Its roots were in Hebrew and Jewish culture, but now it became in principle transcultural, capable of expressing itself in a variety of cultures. In practice, the believers within the Roman Empire were from various ethnic cultures, largely overlaid by late Hellenistic (Greek) culture in the East, and an emerging Latin culture in the West. Those outside Roman rule had other cultures, such as Coptic, Ethiopian, Celtic, or Persian, for example. The long-range implications were that Christianity was potentially a world religion, a faith which could interact with all human cultures. This interaction would later involve adaptations of both the practice of Christianity and the cultures it confronted, as the gospel message produced religious traditions of various types.

Gentile Christianity in the Roman Empire began as a minor sect which was frequently misunderstood and persecuted. In the first three centuries, the members were accused of atheism (not believing in any of the gods), cannibalism (eating the body and blood of Jesus in secret ceremonies), and superstition (believing what others did not believe because of an obscure Galilean preacher). Sometimes they were thrown to the lions or simply beheaded. By the time of Constantine, the first Roman Emperor who claimed this faith, about 10 per cent of the people in his empire had adopted Christianity to be their personal faith.

In the years after 313, when Constantine declared Christianity a licit (lawful) religion, the emperors came to embrace a church–state connection which was to be of great consequence for the history of Christianity in Europe and elsewhere. Constantine had founded a new city named after himself, Constantinople, to rule the Roman Empire, thereafter commonly called the Byzantine Empire. We know the city today as Istanbul, perched on the dividing line between Europe and Asia at the Bosphorus. By the fifth century, Christianity was no longer a persecuted sect, but now a reigning majority, with wealth, status and power.

That position of power was to prove a stumbling block to the growth of Christianity among non-European peoples, who began to associate it with the oppression of Byzantium. Within Europe itself, Christianity gained an imperial status it had not known during its first 300 years of widespread growth. Now it expanded more frequently by royal edict than out of personal conviction. Then it had been dangerous to be a Christian; now it was the socially accepted, or even the required, thing to do. This transition meant that the hardy Christians of the first three centuries, especially the martyrs, were held in high regard by the privileged ones of the next three.

We see in the first six centuries the beginning and development of certain themes in Christian spirituality which are significant to the present day: worship and sacraments, charisms (gifts of the Holy Spirit), witness unto death, spiritual disciplines, monasticism, and mysticism. These were important in both Roman and non-Roman contexts.

Worship and sacraments nourished early Christians

The individualistic assumptions which we bring to spirituality did not apply in the first century. As Judaism developed a congregational form of worship in the synagogues of the diaspora, so Christians, the first of whom were Jews, assumed that public, communal worship was basic to spirituality. Those first Jewish Christians in Jerusalem, we are told in the Acts of the Apostles, attended prayers in the impressive temple built by Herod the Great. But Christians in other places worshipped in the local house of prayer or synagogue.

Most of the basic elements of Christian worship were inherited from the synagogue: prayer, psalms, Scripture reading, sermons, singing. What was added was the weekly meal of bread and wine, which seems to be an adaptation of either the annual Jewish Passover or a rabbi's meal with his disciples, a Kiddush. Partaking of this common meal or Lord's Supper was a celebration of the resurrection of the Master, who had said, 'Do this in remembrance of me.' But this was also seen as participating in the 'body of Christ' and receiving this 'bread of heaven' in a very realistic manner. This Eucharist ('thanksgiving') became the centre of Christian worship.

First as small groups, later as immense congregations in cathedrals, Christians gathered on the first day of the week for prayer, preaching, and the Eucharist. Worship became more elaborate as time passed, but its importance for Christian spirituality was not questioned. Private prayer no doubt had its place, but the social character of the 'body of Christ' meant that common prayer was central.

Baptism as initiation into the community was seen as the end of the old life and the beginning of the new. Some took this to mean that baptism meant the forgiveness of previous sins in the old life, but that the new life was to be perfect, without sin. This led to the postponement of baptism by some who feared that there would be no forgiveness afterward! Deathbed baptisms were not unknown, including the famous case of Constantine himself. The Roman preacher we know as Hermas had tried to dissolve this anxiety about baptism by writing in his book, *The Shepherd*, that there was indeed forgiveness for the baptized. It was not until ritual confession before the assembly was seen as a medicine for the post-baptismal sinner that people began once again to be baptized upon conversion or as infants.

Christian spirituality in the early centuries was communal spirituality, originating in baptism, rooted in the worship of the congregation, and nourished by weekly celebrations of the Supper instituted by Jesus.

Charisms (gifts of the Holy Spirit) showed God's love and power

The 'charismatic' element in Christianity refers to the gifts given to individual Christians for the common good. The Greek word for such a gracious, free gift, is *charisma*. These gifts may include very ordinary acts, such as washing someone's feet or sharing one's food, and extraordinary powers, such as instantly healing a sick person or conveying a specific message from God for a given situation. They are traceable to the earliest days of the church, and are highlighted in both Acts and 1 Corinthians. The twentieth-century Pentecostal and Charismatic movements look back to these roots as expressing essential elements of Christianity.

The book of Acts, probably written in the 80s of the first century, describes the earliest years of the church from the 30s to the 60s, from the departure of Jesus to Paul's arrival in Rome. This account emphasizes the role of the Holy Spirit in the development of the earliest church, by describing the Pentecost event in chapter 2, and by continual references to the power of God's Spirit. This verse is often chosen as a summary of the book:

> But you will receive power when the Holy Spirit has come upon you;
> and you will be my witnesses in Jerusalem, in all Judea and Samaria,
> and to the ends of the earth. [1]

It can be said that living the Christian life and developing the community are not within ordinary human ability. Only when the Spirit, later described as the third person of the Trinity, empowers the disciples does the community grow.

In its first 'honeymoon' after Pentecost, the Jerusalem church lived a communal life, sharing goods. Later the church had more difficulty in overcoming ethnic differences in this sharing, and appointed members of the deprived group who were 'full of the Spirit and wisdom' to oversee the distribution (Acts 6).

Here are a few more examples of the work of the Spirit in Acts. In Acts 2, the Spirit is promised by Peter to those who repent and are baptized. In chapter 4 the Spirit empowers Peter and the whole community to speak 'the word of God with boldness'. Chapters 7 and 8 describe how the Spirit guides Stephen and Philip. Paul, like all other major figures in the early community, is 'filled with the Holy Spirit' in chapter 9. Finally, in chapter 10 we read how the first Gentiles received the Holy Spirit:

> While Peter was still speaking, the Holy Spirit fell upon all who heard the word. The circumcised believers who had come with Peter were astounded that the gift of the Holy Spirit had been poured out even on the Gentiles, for they heard them speaking in tongues and extolling God. Then Peter said, 'Can anyone withhold the water for baptizing these people who have received the Holy Spirit just as we have?' So he ordered them to be baptized in the name of Jesus Christ.[2]

The rather glowing picture of charisms, signs and wonders in Acts must be compared with the more troubled picture which emerges from 1 Corinthians, written in the 50s. Paul writes to a church that is splitting apart, partly because of the spiritual pride of some who exercise charisms. He lists nine charisms in chapter 12, without saying that this is a complete list (compare Romans 12 and Ephesians 4):

> To each is given the manifestation of the Spirit for the common good. To one is given through the Spirit the utterance of wisdom, and to another the utterance of knowledge according to the same Spirit, to another faith by the same Spirit, to another gifts of healing by the one Spirit, to another the working of miracles, to another prophecy, to another the discernment of spirits, to another various kinds of tongues, to another the interpretation of tongues. All these are activated by one and the same Spirit, who allots to each one individually just as the Spirit chooses.[3]

It is clear that the church members in Corinth are misusing their gifts and thus tearing apart the community. In chapter 13 Paul inserts into his discussion of gifts the beautiful and profound hymn to love: 'If I speak in the tongues of men or of angels, but have not love...' This chapter is much better known than his discussion of the charisms in chapters 12 and 14, but the context provided in the surrounding chapters helps us realize that he is talking about the gift of tongues.

Paul does not suggest love as an alternative gift to the others, but as 'a more excellent way' in which the gifts are to be evaluated and exercised. He underlines that the gifts are temporary, while faith, hope and love are eternal. He emphasizes that love means patience, kindness and humility in the exercise of the gifts.

Paul goes on to give specific instructions for worship services in chapter 14. He gives an ambivalent account of speaking in tongues, which is described as praying with the spirit but not with the mind. On the one hand he asserts that this gift is very limited, since it edifies, or builds up, the one who prays in a tongue, but is of no help to anyone else who does not understand it. He says that in church, he would rather speak five words with his mind, than ten thousand words in a tongue. He also suggests that not everyone speaks in tongues, and urges Christians to seek the higher gifts, notably prophecy.

On the other hand, Paul affirms this gift, which seems to be the lowliest by his reckoning. He claims to speak in tongues more than any of them, and says that it is not to be forbidden in the worship service. His implicit message is that speaking in tongues is best exercised in private prayer, where its edifying effect for the individual does not confuse other hearers.

It seems likely that many churches in the first and early second centuries practised a spirituality which encouraged charismatic expression. The remarkable *Odes of Solomon* seem to come from Edessa or Antioch about the year AD100, and express a Syriac spirituality full of praise and love for God.[4] The author or authors are unknown, but the odes may be a hymnbook, comparable to the Psalms, which express a charismatic spirituality full of praise.

> As the work of the ploughman is the ploughshare,
> and the work of the helmsman is the steering of the ship,
> so also my work is the psalm of the Lord in his praises.
> My art and my service are in his praises,
> because his love has nourished my heart,
> and his fruits he poured unto my lips.

For my love is the Lord;
hence I shall sing unto him.
For I am strengthened in his praises,
And I have faith in him.
I shall open my mouth,
and his spirit will speak through me
the praise of the Lord and his beauty.
(16:1–5)[5]

Syriac Christianity used feminine symbols more frequently than did Greek or Latin. As the following quotation will show, the use of female images for God is not just a recent fad in Christianity, but goes back to the early centuries. The Holy Spirit was long identified as female in Syriac spirituality, just as the Hebrew word for spirit is feminine. A strong devotion to the Virgin Mary developed early, including the legend that Mary bore Jesus without pain. This view seems to romanticize the birth of Jesus instead of accepting the down-to-earth character of Mary and the incarnation. Feminine images for God included the breasts of God flowing with milk, a symbol of nourishment and delight. All of these themes can be seen in the remarkable nineteenth Ode of Solomon, which is worth quoting in full:

A cup of milk was offered to me,
and I drank it in the sweetness of the Lord's kindness.
The Son is the cup,
and the Father is he who was milked;
and the Holy Spirit is she who milked him;
Because his breasts were full,
and it was undesirable that his milk should be released
    without purpose.
The Holy Spirit opened her bosom,
and mixed the milk of the two breasts of the Father.
Then she gave the mixture to the generation without
    their knowing,
and those who have received [it] are in the perfection of
    the right hand.
The womb of the Virgin took [it],
and she received conception and gave birth.
So the Virgin became a mother with great mercies.
And she laboured and bore the Son but without pain,

because it did not occur without purpose.
And she did not seek a midwife,
because he caused her to give life.
She bore as a strong man with desire,
and she bore according to the manifestation,
and possessed with great power.
And she loved with salvation,
and guarded with kindness,
and declared with greatness.
Hallelujah.[6]

Following hints from the Old Testament, God is seen as female. Later, several medieval mystics, men and women, would refer to God as Mother, but retain the masculine pronoun, as here in the *Odes of Solomon*. See the discussion of Julian of Norwich in Chapter 4.

The charismatic phenomena of the first century seem largely to disappear in the following centuries. We have evidence concerning this change from a document, the *Didache*, or *Teaching of the Twelve Apostles*, commonly dated early in the second century. It is an anonymous writing, probably from Syria, which shows the structuring of the church out of the more fluid spontaneity of the charismatic period. Just as Paul dealt with problems concerning the use of tongues, this document warns about misuse of prophecy. It warns that travelling prophets should not be allowed to stay in a church for more than three days, lest they falsely fleece the flock.

Thus the sociological demands of better organization made it necessary for the leadership of the churches to become more learned and less spontaneous. Further, it seems from comments by later church fathers, that they did not even know what speaking in tongues was; they had never heard or experienced it.

The Montanists, who were condemned as heretics, had a role to play in the growing disfavour of charismatic phenomena. Followers of **Montanus** (about 157) in Asia Minor emerged in the mid-second century with a 'new prophecy', an expectation of the parousia or return of Christ, and a rigorous set of ethical norms. They were led by Montanus himself and two female assistants, Maximilla and Priscilla. It was charged against them that they allowed women to speak and that Montanus claimed to be the Paraclete, or Counsellor, promised by Jesus in the Gospel of John.

It seems likely that there was deliberate misunderstanding of their teaching. We have today almost no original writings which would give us their own spirituality; we have mainly the charges of their enemies. Much of what they taught was characteristic of the church in general a century earlier. They were not in step with the later replacement of the charisms by offices, easier rules of conduct, and waning of the imminent expectation of the parousia. But the group itself moved in this direction by the third century. Tertullian, whom we will meet later in this chapter, became a Montanist at that time, but it was moral rigour which attracted him, not the exercise of charisms.

At any rate, these gifts continued to be practised on the margins of the church until our own century, when they were rediscovered by Pentecostal and Charismatic groups on all continents (see Chapter 7).

Martyrs witnessed unto death

In Christian tradition the martyr, man or woman, was honoured for holding the faith as being of higher value than life itself, for showing what one ancient writer called 'contempt' for the horrors of death. The root meaning of the word is 'witness', implying that death at the hands of Romans or others was the ultimate testimony of faith. Our modern conception of a 'martyr complex' suggests that the person who dies must be mentally unsound, and that the ultimate value for any healthy person must be one's own life. Others, more thoughtful, see giving one's life for the sake of faith as the ultimate gift of the truly healthy person.

Persecution of Christians began in the New Testament period, and it did not end until Constantine's legitimizing of the faith in 313. Jesus himself had said, 'Take up your cross and follow me.' During the sporadic persecutions by various Roman officials in different parts of the empire, the strength of conviction of Christians was severely tested.

The theme of martyrdom appears among the earliest group of writings after the New Testament, by the so-called 'Apostolic Fathers'. Among them, Bishop **Ignatius of Antioch** (who lived about 160–220 in Syria, Western Asia) writes on the way to Rome, addressing letters to six churches and one bishop (Polycarp) along the way. Clearly his model is Paul, who is thought to have been martyred in Rome about 64. Ignatius' letters have the freshness and personal character of Paul's writing, and often even the phrases of

1 Corinthians and other letters. There is a clear gap, however, between the apostle and his imitator. Ignatius' images, theology and tone do not equal the depth of his mentor.

Ignatius describes his eagerness to die for his faith, asking readers to pray for his steadfastness. At the same time he urges them to be unified and obedient to their own bishops and to avoid heresy, especially the teaching that Jesus did not really experience birth, and death on a cross (Docetism).

'We have not only to be called Christians, but to be Christians', he writes to the Magnesians (4:1). For Ignatius, that clearly implies willingness to die for the sake of the faith. 'If we do not willingly die in union with his Passion, we do not have his life in us' (5:1). It is in the letter to Rome that Ignatius most fervently expresses his desire for martyrdom, imploring them not to intercede and prevent his death. For Ignatius, death in the coliseum means that he will 'get to God'. This is his passionate desire, as the climax of his life on earth.

The world is mostly an enemy according to such a perspective. There is no time for meditating on the beauties of creation in these documents. Rather Ignatius exhorts his readers to fight the good fight, to be faithful to their bishops, and to avoid false teaching.

Another martyr in the early centuries was **Perpetua,** who met her death about AD200 in Carthage. Much of the account of her martyrdom is a first-person account. As the young mother of an infant, she gave up her baby to others' care as she went to the stadium to meet wild beasts and eventually the sword. She defied the authority of Rome, not only to determine her religious practice, but even to choose the clothes in which she would meet her death. Her account of the last days, with a conclusion written perhaps by Tertullian, is one of the rare documents describing martyrdom as it was, and not in rhapsodic and legendary exaggerations.

Martyrdom stands as the ultimate test of any spirituality; it is the feature of discipleship which symbolizes the opposition of the world to Christian devotion as well as the utmost extent of Christian commitment. It indicates a testimony to one's faith which will not deny itself, no matter what human society may do to enforce conformity. Martyrdom might be thought of as a passive act, allowing oneself to be killed. But it is clear that both Ignatius and Perpetua, though they yielded to God's will, assertively refused to evade holy execution. In these cases, martyrdom is action in the world based on the example of Jesus himself.

Christians engaged in asceticism, the practice of disciplines

There are certain disciplines which have long characterized the Christian life. They involve exercise in virtue and avoidance of vice. Together, these disciplines are called *ascesis*, or asceticism. It is a word not often used favourably in our own age. The basic idea is that of athletic training in preparation for a contest, for example, a race. Paul writes,

> Do you not know that in a race the runners all compete, but only one receives the prize? Run in such a way that you may win it. Athletes exercise self-control in all things; they do it to receive a perishable wreath, but we an imperishable one.[7]

The Old Testament records not only a moral code, such as the Ten Commandments, but also special ascetic rules for certain situations, such as abstaining from food, alcohol, haircuts, or sex. In the New Testament, Jesus seems to assume that his followers will fast and give alms as was common in his own day.[8] He speaks in dramatic metaphors about the seriousness of sexual lust.[9] He calls on followers to deny themselves and take up the cross.[10]

In the Hellenistic context, asceticism took on forms that seldom appeared within Judaism. The exaltation of virginity and the life of celibacy, for example, were sometimes motivated by views of the world which replaced the doctrine of creation with a world-weary late Roman despair.

Indeed Paul had recommended celibacy in 1 Corinthians 7. He did so, however, because he believed the time was very short before the return of Christ, and because women and men could devote themselves to the work to be done more wholeheartedly without a family. His discussion is surprisingly balanced in terms of men and women. For example he sees each marriage partner having sexual desires and conjugal rights.[11] But later writers urged celibacy for very different reasons, namely that the body is evil and sex is evil. Then the practice left behind the Jewish and Christian doctrines of creation, and the door was open for vilifying women as the object of the stifled sexual desire of celibate men.

Especially from the late twentieth-century perspective, the early practice of identifying women with sex and sin must be seen as very damaging to Christian spirituality. Asceticism was widespread in many cultures, not just

Hellenistic ones, suggesting that it has a basic role in Christian spirituality, but that it was misinterpreted or exaggerated in given situations.

Ascetic practices, in my opinion, can be healthy or unhealthy. In a Christian context they need to meet two criteria for wholesomeness. First, do they affirm the goodness of creation? Is the motivation to free the person for better service, to give up something good for something better? If not, it may be a denial of the goodness of creation, of the body, sometimes of the goodness of sexuality.

The second criterion, in my view, is whether the grace of God is being replaced by human effort. Is this effort made in order to earn the love of God, which cannot be earned, because it is flowing towards us freely and unconditionally? Or is it a response to God's forgiving grace in Christ? Does the practice lead to the freedom of the athlete who runs in the knowledge of God's love, or to the bondage of a desperate attempt to earn what cannot be earned? Or is it even self-punishment to atone for sins which Christ has already forgiven?

Three early Christian theologians who wrote in different languages, nevertheless agreed on the importance of ascetic disciplines for the Christian life. Origen and Tertullian were both from Africa, Ephrem from Asia. Origen, who wrote in Greek, became head of a famous catechetical school in Alexandria, following his master Clement. Tertullian, a lawyer in Carthage (near today's Tunis) was among the first Christian writers in Latin. Because of their strong influence upon the development of later Christianity, I will write at some length about these two men, and then touch briefly on the Syriac writer, Ephrem.

In **Tertullian** (160?–225) we hear the voice of the rigourist, one who exhorts the Christian to separation from the world. As a Catholic, before he turned to the rigour of the Montanist heresy, he wrote 'To the Martyrs', 'Spectacles', and 'The Apparel of Women'. Each of these ascetical writings demands separation from the pagan world of Carthage, North Africa, in about AD200.

He tells the (potential) martyrs that they are better off in prison than in the world, since the world itself is a vast prison with disgusting moral rot and seductive temptations all about ('To the Martyrs', chapter 2). He argues with great dialectical skill against Christian attendance at the games and plays that are dedicated to pagan gods and exhibit no respect for human life or chaste morals ('Spectacles'). And finally he urges women to dress modestly, not in gold and make-up, as God did not intend it and there is no rational ground for such 'lust' to please others. In these three essays (sermons) Tertullian makes clear that to him, a commitment to Christian spirituality meant a sharp break from 'the world, the flesh and the devil' (the gods of the pagans).

His discussion of pleasure in 'Spectacles' (the general name for the various performances in Roman amphitheatres; 28–29), is instructive. There people were exposed naked for all to ogle, and bloodlust was encouraged by fights to the death.

> And finally, if you think that you are to pass this span of life in delights, why are you so ungrateful as not to be satisfied with so many and so exquisite pleasures given you by God, and not to recognize them? For what is more delightful than reconciliation with God, our Father and Lord, than the revelation of truth, the recognition of past errors, and pardon for such grievous sins of the past? What greater pleasure is there than distaste of pleasure itself, than contempt of all the world can give, than true liberty, than a pure conscience, than a contented life, than freedom from fear of death? To trample underfoot the gods of the heathen, to drive out demons, to effect cures, to seek revelations, to live unto God—these are the pleasures, these are the spectacles of the Christians, holy, everlasting and free of charge.[12]

Tertullian does have a point, that Christians may not notice or acknowledge the pleasures they experience by the practice of their faith. But what is missing here is any sense of the small, daily pleasures of life—looking at flowers, listening to music, making love with one's spouse, creative writing, physical labour, etc. To put it briefly, Tertullian has missed the joys of the created order in his description of 'Christian' pleasures. Only the 'spiritual' pleasures remain, as a foil to the artificial, often immoral pleasures of the spectacles which Rome provided for an increasingly callous populace.

Tertullian laid the foundations for Latin doctrinal theology. As one of the first Latin authors who had an intellectual grasp of the Christian message, he forged new terms, such as 'Old Testament', 'New Testament', 'Trinity', and 'person' (to describe each member of the Trinity). His influence on Latin writers after him was immense, and he was a major contributor to the eventual orthodox view of the Trinity.

Tertullian seemed to reject Greek philosophical influence in Christian theology. He asked, 'What does Athens have to do with Jerusalem?' His point was that genuine teaching came from Christ, not from the speculations of the Gnostics who seemed to gain their inspiration from the Greek philosophers. In this regard he was not influential, because for centuries much of the Christian theology of the Roman Empire was a synthesis of Hebrew and Greek thought.

The Good News does need contextualization, that is, expression within a cultural context which is authentic to that culture. For example, Africans today have the right and responsibility to think through the Christian message and express its implications in words (preaching, theology, prayers) and artistic expression (sculpture, dance, music) which is thoroughly African.

Tertullian's question, however, may be taken as a warning for all later Christians. He calls for an evaluation of Christian teaching to see if it is true to its sources, or has been influenced by some other way of thinking which distorts it. The tendency to ignore aspects of the message which challenge our assumptions is very strong when adapting the Christian message to one's own culture. Has the genuine gospel message been distorted by cultural adaptation? Have North Americans, for example, so interpreted the Christian message that it does not challenge their affluence in a world of poverty? In our day he might ask, 'What does Madison Avenue have to do with Jerusalem?'

Tertullian eventually decided that even the Catholic Church was not rigorous enough for him. He joined the Montanists, discussed above, whose standards of behaviour were even stricter than those of the church. He came to believe that there was no forgiveness of sin after baptism and that widows and widowers should not remarry. Tertullian's ascesis was sincere, consistent, and within the bounds of orthodoxy for much of his life. Yet he missed some very important themes in what we would consider a balanced ascesis or spirituality today. He seems to miss the generosity of God in forgiveness, the wonder of the good creation, and the need for authentic contextualizing.

Origen (185–254), his younger contemporary, was intrigued by ideas, and is known as the first Christian 'systematic theologian'. That is, he sought to create a rationally satisfying system of thought which embodied Christian understandings of the world and God. He, like Tertullian, was eventually influential in the doctrine of the Trinity, but his approach was considerably different.

He worked within the context of Hellenism, that is, Greek culture as spread by Alexander the Great and his successors. Origen lived in the intellectual centre of Hellenism, in Alexandria (named for Alexander the Great). His question became—given the sort of world-view first developed by Plato and later developed by Plotinus ('Neo-Platonism')—how could one understand the Christian Scriptures?

Origen set himself the task of examining in great detail the Hebrew and Christian Scriptures. His *Hexapla* was an immense project, listing six different texts side by side for detailed comparison. Origen also wrote commentaries and preached homilies on much of the Bible. In spite of this biblical interest, Origen seems to be controlled by his philosophical assumptions rather than by his biblical studies. In 553, long after his death, Origen was condemned as a heretic.

Yet his influence continued, especially through monks who found that his spiritual teachings outweighed any questions about his orthodoxy in doctrine. This spiritual teaching focused on martyrdom, prayer and Scripture. It saw the spiritual life as an ascent to God, much as Plotinus, the Hellenistic philosopher, had envisioned it.

Origen postulated a fall of rational beings before the creation, which resulted in human souls living in this world. That is, each of us was thought to have a pre-existence, in which we somehow moved away from God. The goal of human life is to return to God, and in fact Origen believed that all humans would so return. These beliefs were among the most controversial, leading to his later condemnation.

The days of the martyrs were far from over in Origen's day. His own father was martyred in 203, and Origen himself wanted to offer his life to the authorities at age sixteen. Thanks be to his mother! She hid his clothes. Without trousers he was too embarrassed to go out of the house, and one of the greatest Christian thinkers was saved for another day. Later Origen did in fact die from the effects of torture inflicted because of his faith, and is rightly called a martyr.

Origen set forth a three-stage schema for the Christian life which in later forms was to become normative for centuries to come. He spoke of moral, natural and contemplative levels. These are not totally exclusive or sequential, but nevertheless refer to stages of development. The moral level has to do with behaviour and can be compared to the book of Proverbs. Secondly the natural level is related to intellectual, observational activity, which is reflected in Ecclesiastes. Finally the contemplative level refers to the spiritual union with God, exemplified in the Song of Songs (read allegorically, that is, as a love song between God and the church).

Later the 'purgative, illuminative and unitive stages' of spiritual growth, influenced by Neo-Platonism, would reflect this teaching of Origen. He influenced Gregory of Nyssa, who was a later theologian, and 'Dionysius' (discussed later in this chapter) and much of Eastern and Western monasticism.

The Latin and Greek languages used by Tertullian and Origen were not the only forms of early Christian spiritual writing. Syriac, a later development of Aramaic, the language of Jesus, was used in the Middle East, both within the Roman Empire and east of its borders. It is a language much less familiar to Western scholars than Greek and Latin. Yet some of the important developments and documents of early Christianity are preserved for us only in Syriac.

Syriac spirituality developed differently from that in cultures further west. It is more closely related to Judaism, a Semitic culture, although sometimes influenced by Hellenism. It became extremely ascetic. The anchorites (hermits) in the Syrian desert used their creativity in thinking up bizarre ways to demonstrate their contempt for comfort and the ways of the world. Most famous was Simon Stylites, who lived on a pillar. Others found different ways, living in logs, not bathing, falling on their faces. But later writers tried to moderate the extremes.

Of special interest is **St Ephrem** (306?–73), whose works were copied long after his death by Syrian monks. Ephrem expressed his teachings in symbolic poetry which is still powerful today. He was a deacon in the town of Nisibis, on the border of the Roman Empire, today in south-eastern Turkey. The last decade of his life was lived in exile, after the victorious Persians insisted that all Christians leave Nisibis. He did much of his writing in Edessa, just west of Nisibis. One of the few events of his life of which we know is his service to victims of famine. In the last year of his life, he arranged for 300 beds and food for the homeless and dying, personally serving their needs.

Ephrem advocated virginity not because he despised the flesh, as some of the Greek writers seem to have done. Rather the grounds for his asceticism were marriage with the Bridegroom, the goal of wakefulness, and the ideals of Paradise.[13]

The differences between these two approaches, Hellenic and Semitic, can be well illustrated if one visualizes a circle with a point in the centre, where the point represents the object of theological inquiry; the philosophical tradition of theology will seek to define, to set *horoi*, 'boundaries' or 'definitions', to this central point, whereas St Ephrem's Semitic approach through his poetry will provide a series of paradoxical statements situated as it were at opposite points on the circumference of the circle: the central point is left undefined, but something of its nature can be inferred by joining up the various points around the circumference. St Ephrem is always very insistent that, since the centre point representing the aspect of God's being under discussion stands outside creation, it thus lies beyond the ability of the created intellect to comprehend—and any claim to be able to do so is blasphemous. In all this St Ephrem is obviously very much in harmony with the apophatic tradition of later Greek theology.[14]

The learned St Basil had a great respect for Ephrem, and it is perhaps through Basil that the apophatic approach, which I will discuss later, became so influential. One point to notice here is that spirituality does not always follow from theology, but theology can follow from spirituality. Here is a sample of Ephrem's verse, in fuller expression of an apophatic approach to God.

> If someone concentrates his attention solely
>   on the metaphors used of God's majesty,
> he abuses and misrepresents that majesty,
>   and thus errs
> by means of those metaphors
>   with which God had clothed Himself for his benefit,
> and he is ungrateful to that Grace
>   which stooped low
> to the level of his childishness:
>   although it has nothing in common with him,
> yet Grace clothed itself in his likeness
>   in order to bring him to the likeness of itself.
>
> Do not let your intellect
>   be disturbed by mere names,
> for Paradise has simply clothed itself
>   in terms that are akin to you;

> it is not because it is impoverished
> > that it put on your imagery;
> rather, your nature is far too weak to be able
> to attain to its greatness,
> > and its beauties are much diminished
> by being depicted in the pale colours
> > with which you are familiar.[15]

Like many later theologians of the East, Ephrem saw the whole process of the Christian life as *theosis*, or divinization. This term was clearly expressed only once in the New Testament: 'that... you may participate in the divine nature'.[16] But theosis was understood to underlie the New Testament message, and became the basis for much Eastern spirituality. Here is a sample from Ephrem and a comment from Sebastian Brock, an expert on Syriac spirituality:

> Divinity flew down and descended
> > to raise and draw up humanity.
> The Son has made beautiful the servant's deformity,
> > and he has become a god, just as he desired.

It has sometimes been said that the concept of the divinization, or *theosis*, of humanity is something that crept into Christianity, and especially Eastern Christianity, under Hellenic influence. It is clear, however, that St Ephrem, whom Theodoret described as 'un-acquainted with the language of the Greeks', and whose thought patterns are essentially Semitic and Biblical in character, is none-theless an important witness to this teaching.[17]

I have discussed the asceticism of Tertullian, Origen and Ephrem, to show my conviction that asceticism is a valid aspect of Christian spirituality. However it is sometimes but not always based on a rejection of the fourth relationship in the model used in this book: our relation to creation. An extreme asceticism leads to despising God's good gifts of creation: our bodies and the world around us. A legalistic asceticism leads to despising God's grace in favour of personal merit. But a biblical asceticism leads to a healthy sense of being able to say 'no' to a good thing for the sake of a better or higher one; it gives self-confidence while enabling people to serve others.

Monasticism spread from Egypt to the Celts of Britain and Ireland

Africa was the scene of experiments in spiritual life which have shaped both the Western and Eastern traditions ever since. It was in Egypt that men and women first entered the desert to live out more fully the ascetical life they longed for, but the practice quickly spread to Asia and Europe.

Among the first was **Antony of Egypt** (about 250–353) whose *Life* was described by **Athanasius** (296?–373), Bishop of Alexandria. Although Antony was a Copt, one of the people of ancient Egypt, and Athanasius was of Hellenist background, they came to know each other when Athanasius was exiled, running for protection from the emperor's soldiers to the monks of the desert. Athanasius adhered stubbornly to the full divinity of Christ as stated in the Nicene Creed of 325. He suffered five exiles from opponents of the idea that Christ was of 'one Being with the Father'.

The Life of Antony tells the story of Antony's beginnings in the ascetical life after the death of his parents. He heard the gospel read in church, 'Sell all that you have and give it to the poor.' Immediately he did so, and renouncing economic power, entered into training with others who knew this path, learning something from each one. A crucial step was Antony's dwelling in a tomb, the place of death, and overcoming everything that the powers of death could throw at him. Although taken for dead himself, he returned to the tomb from a 'wake' at which his body was laid out among the mourners, to finally outlast the powers of the demons. The description of his struggle in the tomb includes Antony's rescue by Christ, who in Antony's experience (and in Athanasius' theology) was the victorious conqueror of death and demons.

Then Antony penetrated deeper and deeper into the desert, carrying his offensive to the opponents' 'home territory'. It was understood at that time that the desert was the dwelling-place of the devil and his minions. Recall that Jesus too had confronted Satan in the desert. Antony gave his whole time and energy to the struggle. Like other monks he laboured for his living, but also spent his time meditating on memorized Scripture. Many people came to him for advice and help.

Antony's life exhibits not only discipline but tenderness and service. He not only lived the utterly simplified life of a hermit but also advised, reconciled, healed, and encouraged those who sought his aid. He did not so much escape from the world as engage the enemy of humankind in spiritual combat. Antony went forth in the power of the cross to defeat Satan through Christ's victory. In doing so, he forged a new style of Christian spiritual life, the monastic. He was not the first monk in the world, but he was among the very first who entered the far desert with specifically Christian motivations.

The sayings of many who followed Antony's example, the desert fathers and mothers (yes, women went out into the desert too!), have been collected and translated in many editions.[18] They have given insight into the spare, clean and rugged life of the desert which has been a potent challenge and encouragement to all who seek a singleness of vision in our own day. Here are some samples of the short stories and words remembered from the Egyptian mothers:

> [Amma (Mother) Theodora] also said, that neither asceticism, nor vigils nor any kind of suffering are able to save, only true humility can do that. There was an anchorite who was able to banish the demons; and he asked them, 'What makes you go away? Is it fasting?' They replied, 'We do not eat or drink.' 'Is it vigils?' They replied, 'We do not sleep.' 'Is it separation from the world?' 'We live in the deserts.' 'What power sends you away then?' They said, 'Nothing can overcome us, but only humility.' 'Do you see how humility is victorious over the demons?'[19]

> [Sarah] also said to the brothers, 'It is I who am a man, you who are women.'[20]

> [Blessed Syncletica] also said, 'If you find yourself in a monastery do not go to another place, for that will harm you a great deal. Just as the bird who abandons the eggs she was sitting on prevents them from hatching, so the monk or the nun grow cold and their faith dies, when they go from one place to another.'[21]

> She also said, 'As long as we are in the monastery, obedience is preferable to asceticism. The one teaches pride, the other humility...' Amma Syncletica said, 'There are many who live in the mountains and behave as if they were in the town, and they are wasting their time. It is possible to be a solitary in one's mind while living in a crowd, and it is possible for one who is a solitary to live in the crowd of his own thoughts.'[22]

The first experiments with communal monasticism, as opposed to the individual or anchorite type practised by Antony, were accomplished by Pachomius, also in the Egyptian desert. But the most influential founders of this type of monasticism were Basil of Caesarea in the East, that is the Greek-speaking half of the Mediterranean basin, and Benedict of Nursia in the West, the Latin-speaking part of the empire, increasingly centred in Rome.

In the East, **Basil of Caesarea** (330–79), from what is today Turkey, was a major influence on monasticism. A strong belief in the superiority of communal monasticism led Basil to write two monastic Rules. His emphases were on the whole of life as thanksgiving, on the spiritual gifts, and the importance of obedience in attacking self-will. The whole process of growth or sanctification is the process of restoring the image of God, lost by the first parents. Basil defended trinitarian doctrine, just as Athanasius before him. He was influential in asserting the full divinity of the Holy Spirit and the final acceptance of the Nicene Creed at Constantinople in 381. However, he was also influenced by the earlier Alexandrian, Origen, and selected some of Origen's writings for the original collection of spiritual writings named the *Philokalia* (the love of beauty, parallel to 'philosophy', the love of wisdom). Later we will discuss another, much larger *Philokalia* collected in the eighteenth century. Basil's own spiritual teaching, unlike that of Origen, leads from light into divine darkness, rather than from darkness into divine light. This surprising reversal is more fully developed by Pseudo-Dionysius, discussed at the end of this chapter.

Basil had two associates, who worked with him: Gregory of Nyssa (his brother) and Gregory of Nazianzus (his friend). Together the three are known as the Cappadocian Fathers, after the region of Cappadocea in Asia Minor. All shared a commitment to the Nicene Creed, but each had different gifts. Basil was the organizer, the bishop, the abbot. Gregory of Nyssa was the most gifted intellectually. And Gregory of Nazianzus was most eloquent. Macrina, Basil and Gregory of Nyssa's sister, influenced them greatly.[23]

Evagrius of Pontus (345?–99) is an important link between the Cappadocians and later writers, especially monks, Eastern and Western. He knew the Cappadocians personally, but he also travelled to Egypt and lived in the desert there. His teaching was influenced most strongly by Origen and to a lesser degree by Gregory of Nazianzus, and he became a Christian Platonist, following the lines of the philosophy developed by Plato. Though he was later condemned with Origen, his teachings circulated anonymously or under other names. It is striking that heretical writers were so influential in medieval Christian spirituality!

The goal of life, according to Evagrius, is the recovery of the knowledge of God and the unity of rational spirits, lost in the primordial fall. The Christian life has 'stages': the practical, natural and theological. He analysed the dangers to the Christian life to be eight in number. These were later pared down to seven by John Cassian and became the 'seven deadly sins'. Evagrius' list included gluttony, lust, avarice, dejection, anger, despondency (*akedia* or 'accidie'), vainglory and pride.[24]

Apatheia (passionlessness or freedom from passion) was for Evagrius the healthy functioning of the soul's powers. It was the desirable state for Christians, but not the only goal of Christian living. He thought that the goal of prayer was a stripping of the mind, a pure consciousness of God without images or thoughts. This would restore the lost knowledge of God.

John Cassian (about 360–432) took Evagrius' teachings to the West. He knew Evagrius in Egypt, then travelled to Marseilles, where he founded a monastery. He wrote a number of books, including his *Conferences* which reflected what he had learned from the Egyptian monks, especially Evagrius. These readings were canonized by Benedict for reading by monks, and thus came to be commonly accepted in the West. The ideas were basically those of Evagrius but now in the context of Gaul and in Latin language. John Cassian was a cross-cultural transmitter of the ideals of the Origenist stream of Egyptian monasticism.

In the West, in Italy, **Benedict** (about 480–547) founded the Benedictine Order, still one of the largest Catholic religious communities. After experiments with solitude, he came to develop a system of monastic governance which gave the abbot a great deal of authority while insisting on mutual discussion and advice. His *Rule* is relatively brief and non-legalistic: the basic principles are set down without trying to settle all cases in advance.

One of the fundamental spiritual principles of the *Rule* is the incorporation of physical labour with prayer. The motto is *Ora et Labora*. The rhythm of prayers seven times each day interspersed with physical labour, eating and sleeping in moderation, became the norm for Western monks up to the present day.

Benedict also prescribed *lectio divina*, or sacred reading, for four hours each day. (See the spiritual exercise for chapter 2 in Appendix 2.) Monks were to read the Scriptures and the early Christian writers, then meditate on them in silence or while working (six hours daily). He praised silence as a virtue. How far we have come from his ideals today, with constant noise, and little time to concentrate, think and meditate, even in church!

The vows taken by monks and nuns in succeeding centuries are not defined in Benedict's *Rule*, but they reflect his influence. Vows of poverty, chastity, obedience and stability are intended as forms of spiritual discipline which make possible a life of community. Poverty by choice is a way of loosening the bonds of possessions which Jesus had warned about. Chastity, in this case, celibacy (not having sexual intimacy with anyone), was intended to loose one from sexual bonding for community service. Obedience is perhaps the hardest of these disciplines, and the one most emphasized by Benedict, for it implies bending the will to another, namely the abbot. This humble renunciation of one's own will to another human being was intended to show the submission of the Christian to God. It is clear that the abbot carried a heavy responsibility in Benedict's plan. Stability refers to remaining in the same monastery for one's whole life, as opposed to wandering around to look for the best one.

Among the early Christian spiritualities, perhaps none has gained so much present-day interest and devotion as the Celtic tradition, which was largely monastic as well. The Celts, a people who had moved from central Europe to settle in Ireland, Scotland, Wales, and western France, were known to the ancient Greeks as 'Keltoi'. They were the people north of the Roman Empire who were considered barbarians. Anyone who has read the Asterix books knows the Gauls who resisted Roman occupation; these Gauls were one branch of the Celts. The Britons, who were later conquered by the Romans, were also Celts, and it is among them that the earliest Christians were found in Great Britain. Aside from the legends of Glastonbury concerning the arrival of Joseph of Arimathea in Britain, there is archaeological evidence in the British Museum of Christians in England in the first few centuries. After the Romans left in the early 400s, the Angles and Saxons pushed the Celtic peoples westward to Cornwall, Wales and Ireland.

What is not common knowledge is that there were Christians in Britain long before St Augustine of Canterbury arrived about 600, and even before **St Patrick** (389?–461?) who is the national saint of Ireland. Patrick, who had come from a Christian family possibly in Wales, had been captured and sent as a slave to Ireland, where he was put to work herding cattle. During this time he had an experience of God, and reports that he prayed a hundred times a day. Patrick found a way to escape, and following an experience of a call from God, he returned to Ireland as a missionary and convinced the women and men powerful in Celtic society of the power of the Trinity. We have very little exact knowledge of Patrick but many legends survive. The following *lorica* (breastplate) is attributed to him.

> I arise today
>> through God's strength to pilot me:
>> God's might to uphold me,
>> God's wisdom to guide me,
>> God's eye to look before me,
>> God's ear to hear me,
>> God's word to speak for me,
>> God's hand to guard me,
>> God's way to lie before me,
>> God's shield to protect me,
>> God's host to secure me
>>> against snares of devils,
>>> against temptations of vices,
>>> against inclinations of nature,
>>> against everyone who shall wish me ill,
>>> afar and anear,
>>> alone and in a crowd.[25]

Some writers have seen connections between the spirituality of Patrick and of later Welsh spirituality, as expressed in the hymnody of William Williams Pantycelin (1717–91). The Welsh have been known for their strong tradition of singing the faith. This came to be a major expression of the Welsh evangelical revivals of the 1800s. In the middle of the nineteenth century most of the population identified with 'chapels' of Methodist or Presbyterian persuasion rather than with the 'Church' of Wales (Anglican).

From the start, monasticism was important to Celtic adherents of the new faith. It seems that there was a direct influence from the Coptic monks of Egypt, and *The Life of Antony* was well-known. The church was headed by abbots rather than bishops. 'Double' monasteries were founded, including both women and men, and sometimes were headed by a woman. The most famous of the women saints of Ireland, **Brigid**, (also known as Bride, Bridget, or Ffraid—died about 523) was such an abbess. According to legend she was most generous, giving away her father's sword, and was ordained a bishop(!) by the leading of the Spirit. An order of St Brigid continues to revere her today in Kildare, Ireland.

Irish Christians lifted the concept of the *anamchara* or 'soul friend' to importance in their spirituality.[26] One was not alone in the Christian walk, but the close companion could encourage and correct one along the way. This was a relationship for counsel, confession, and support, which finds biblical precedent in the words of James in the New Testament: 'Therefore confess your sins to one another and pray for one another, so that you may be healed'.[27]

Like Syriac monasticism, the religious in Ireland were extremely strict in their asceticism. The practice of reciting all 150 Psalms daily was common, and some stood praying in icy water. They spoke of white martyrdom, the daily ascetic practice, red martyrdom, the shedding of blood, and blue martyrdom, the doing of significant penance for sin. Although there was apparently no 'red martyrdom' in the transition from pagan to Christian faith in Ireland, there certainly were Celtic martyrs in England and Wales. The first of these was **St Alban** (died in 209 or 305), a Briton, who gave refuge to a Christian priest when Christianity was persecuted by a Roman emperor (scholars argue whether it was Diocletian or Septimius Severus). Alban was converted and baptized by the priest, then offered himself to the soldiers by wearing the priest's clothing. Eventually both he and the priest were executed.

St Winifred (or Gwenfrewi, in Welsh—died about 650) is also in some sense a martyr. According to legend, she refused the offer of marriage, and was decapitated by her suitor; fortunately, her uncle, St Bueno, was on hand to replace her severed head, so that she lived to found a nunnery on the spot. This spot, in Holywell, is the site of a well which has drawn hundreds and thousands of pilgrims down through the centuries. Among the continuities between Celtic religion and Christianity are the many wells which became associated with Christian saints, and continued to be a symbol of the feminine in spirituality and a practical aid to the sick and wounded. A taste of medieval devotion to St Winifrid can be enjoyed in the mystery novels about Brother Cadfael of Shrewsbury, written by Ellis Peters.

A distinctive feature of Celtic spirituality which later spread to all Roman Catholicism was the practice of private confession (as opposed to public confession) with fixed penances for given offences. Confessional books called *penitentials* prescribed the penance to be paid for a given sin. Later when Irish monks converted many Germanic peoples on the continent, this practice was extended to them. After the Lateran Council of 1215 it became a required practice in Catholic churches to confess to a priest. Later, at the Council of Trent in the mid-1500s, penance was defined as one of the seven sacraments. This sacrament was amended after Vatican II in our own century to eliminate the quantitative approach which had become characteristic, and to give more freedom of practice. Nowadays the renamed Sacrament of Reconciliation is probably closer to the original Celtic practice than was the enumerating of sins in the confessional, characteristic of the period from Trent to Vatican II.

Another distinctive form of asceticism was self-exile from one's home or monastery. It came to be common for Irish monks to leave home as Abraham had been called to do and live far from the community that had nurtured them. This travelling led indirectly to the spread of Christianity in northern Europe.

Among the exiles was **St Columba** (521–97), who landed on the Scottish island of Iona in 563. He is said to have slaughtered 5,000 men and wished to do penance by saving as many among the pagan Scots. Iona became a mission station, and may have been the location of one of the most beautiful manuscripts ever created: the *Book of Kells*. This illustrated biblical masterpiece was taken back home to Ireland for safety from Viking attack. It is a symbol not only of the artistry of the monks but of their devotion to a life of learning. Many students from the Continent came to Ireland to study with its scholar-saints. Today Iona is the home of an ecumenical Christian community founded in the 1930s which emphasizes Christian living in one's calling, including prayer, meditation and social service. I am among the pilgrims who have travelled to Iona for retreats in the restored Abbey, amidst Celtic crosses which predate the Viking era.

The Celtic crosses have a circle connecting the arms and the stem, and the more elaborate ones have carvings in stone of the whole biblical story, centred in Jesus. Some, as at Monasterboice in Ireland, include Paul of Thebes and Antony of Egypt. The many crosses, which still stand in Ireland, Scotland and Wales, are the lasting artistic legacy, along with the biblical manuscripts, of Celtic spirituality.

One of the sources of our knowledge of this spirituality is a collection of prayers made by Alexander Carmichael in the late 1800s called the *Carmina Gadelica*. It is the oral tradition preserved in the Outer Hebrides, that long string of islands in the north west of Scotland. These hymns and prayers give us a unique window into the daily practice of Celtic spirituality, behind the great achievements of the manuscripts and the crosses. They express a sense of God's immediate presence in daily life. Although God is revered as a great King or Chief, it is clear that God is also a close companion. Here is a sample of a poem prayer, including a characteristic repetitive style and an emphasis on the Trinity, but a distinctive good humour as well.

> My walk this day with God,
> My walk this day with Christ,
> My walk this day with Spirit,
>   The Threefold all-kindly:
>   Ho! ho! ho! the Threefold all-kindly.
>
> My shielding this day from ill,
> My shielding this night from harm,
> Ho! ho! both my soul and my body,
>   Be by Father, by Son, by Holy Spirit:
>   By Father, by Son, by Holy Spirit.
>
> Be the Father shielding me,
> Be the Son shielding me,
> Be the Spirit shielding me,
>   As Three and as One:
>   Ho! ho! ho! as Three and as One.[28]

The attractiveness of Celtic Christian spirituality for today is due to at least three authentic factors and to two others which are much more dubious. The first is its unifying character as a style of spirituality with direct links to the Middle East, which preceded the splits of denominations which have daunted the churches. It provides a sort of alternative to Roman or Protestant Christianity, in a setting where Christianity was fresh and unencumbered with ecclesiastical bureaucracy.

Secondly, it is a spirituality which rejoices in the natural world. The first article of the creed comes alive for Celtic spirituality not only in the terrifying beauty of the wind, the rocks and sea, but also in the everyday reliance on God's blessing on the cow, the fire and the bed.

Finally, it is a spirituality affirming of women. The Celtic society included practices which ensured that women would have a major influence on group decisions. St Brigid is a major figure in Irish spirituality, one of the 'trinity' of saints (the other two are Patrick and Columba).

Some people today are attracted to Celtic spirituality because they see in it a rosy view of sunshine without shadow, praise without asceticism, creation without the cross. They must be highly selective to sustain such a view. Celtic spirituality clearly includes the darkness, pain and severe ascetic discipline; it sees the cross of Christ as the key to understanding the victory of God over the powers of evil.

It is also fashionable for some to see Celtic Christianity as entirely separate from the Roman Catholic Christianity of the Continent. In fact, Welsh Celts were very much in contact with the Gauls and Romans, and used the Latin language. Although the Celtic ways were different from Continental ones, they followed earlier Roman traditions, such as the date of Easter. The Celtic Christians never disavowed their allegiance to Rome; they only differed in their traditions.

There remain good reasons for people who are not ethnically Celtic to honour the Celtic tradition and to learn from it for today. It affirms the glory of God in the natural world, it honours women, it lives in daily contact with the divine. To follow and not to romanticize is the challenge faced by today's lover of Celtic tradition.

Another example of the importance of Christian monasticism was in the area we now know as Ethiopia. Christianity had been declared the religion of the kingdom of Axum (or Aksum) in the fourth century. This occurred because two students travelling from Tyre to India were shipwrecked on the Red Sea coast near the capital. The king put them in charge of educating his children, and around AD330 King Ezana became a Christian. One of those students, Frumentius, was named the first bishop. He was consecrated by Athanasius in Alexandria. From that time until 1951 the Abuna or chief bishop was named by the Coptic bishop in Alexandria.

But the evangelization of the peoples of Ethiopia was not accomplished by the king. It was the Nine Saints, each from a different country, who arrived in 480, and spread the faith through monastic houses. They set about the huge task of translating the Bible into the Ge'ez language, one of the oldest biblical translations. They also translated *The Life of Antony* and the *Rule* of Pachomius. In fact these saints had lived in Pachomius' monastery before coming to Ethiopia.

The Ethiopian church grew and developed, in contact with the Byzantine churches until the Arab conquest of the seventh century. Then it was shut off from Red Sea trade, became isolated, and moved inland within present-day Ethiopia.

Today members of the Ethiopian Orthodox Church are expected to fast many days in the year and to pray seven times daily. Prayer is commonly said while standing, with complete prostrations at the beginning and end. The *debteras* or choristers sing at joyful festivals while dancing solemnly with long sticks. Some of these practices may go all the way back to the ancient monks who founded Ethiopian Christianity.

Mysticism developed in East and West

Mysticism is a term much used and misused. Its boundaries are not well-defined, and the reader must always ask in what sense the term is used in order to understand the writer's meaning. The word comes from ancient Greek religion and its root meaning is 'secret'. The participants in rites of the Greek pantheon were not to divulge the proceedings to outsiders. Eventually everything mysterious was connected with 'mysticism'.

The term is an elastic one, used by different writers in different ways. In general, mysticism is a form of spirituality which sets as its goal unity with God (or, in some religions, with the Ultimate). Mystics generally have reached a level of contemplation at which they cannot describe their experiences, but use colourful language and poetry to convey the gist of it to those who have not experienced their ecstasy. They tend to see the whole world as charged with divine glory, and sometimes actively change the world by their vision of justice and love.

The essential meaning of mysticism in the Christian tradition is the experience of God as One with whom we have union or communion. The terms 'union' and 'communion' are extremely important. Union with God can mean complete absorption, ultimately losing one's identity in God. It can be argued that such a view goes against the grain of orthodox Christian teaching, for it suggests that ultimately there is no self, and therefore redemption and moral responsibility become null and void. If there is no redeemed person then Christianity loses its basic view of the world.

Communion, on the other hand, suggests a kind of loving relationship of two persons who remain distinct in spite of a unity of purpose, feeling and/or knowledge. Christian mystics have had a great deal of difficulty articulating their experiences of God, and most have spoken of union with God. Whether the term is to be understood in an absolute sense, as above, or in the modified sense of communion must be determined in each individual case. Often 'union' is used in the sense of communion, but it may be ambiguous.

Two of the most influential writers of the early period wrote in a mystical vein. They came from opposite ends of the empire and their teachings were in very different modes. They are Augustine of Hippo in North Africa and 'Dionysius the Areopagite', probably from Syria.

Augustine of Hippo (354–430), the celebrated author of the *Confessions*, gave a narrative character to Christian growth which had not been present before. It was a brand new concept: a book which narrates one's inner life with God. Augustine addresses God throughout the book, confessing both sin and faith. He tells his story in a conversation with God which leads him to appreciate God's love for him every step of the way.

In reconstructing his past, he was searching out the ways God had been seeking him, and seeing that what happened was not entirely in his own power. The sense of being in the hands of forces greater than oneself is very strong and the narrative character of the understanding brings down to earth some of the principles and proverbs of the Egyptian monks. It was the story of Antony of Egypt which led to Augustine's final break with his old life and the turning to a new one.

The whole of the *Confessions* testifies to a personal longing for God, finally satisfied. Tracing his early years, Augustine tells of his mother Monica, a devout Christian who became the most influential person in his life, and his father Patricius, not a Christian. He recalls his unhappiness in school, his attraction to Manichaeism, a religion setting the matter of the world as an evil opponent to the good spiritual God, and his departure from it. Having become a teacher of rhetoric, Augustine seeks his fortune in Rome and Milan. There he finds the framework for all his subsequent thought in late forms of Plato's philosophy and is convinced by the preaching of Bishop Ambrose that one does not have to commit intellectual suicide to believe the Bible.

Finally in a famous scene in a garden, he gives up the struggle and gives in to God. Hearing children nearby singing 'Take up and read', he read from Romans 13:13–14: 'let us live honourably as in the day, not in revelling and drunkenness, not in debauchery and licentiousness, not in quarrelling and jealousy. Instead, put on the Lord Jesus Christ, and make no provision for the flesh, to gratify its desires.'

Since Augustine had been living with a concubine, this verse seemed pointed at him. His sexual life with her had been the obstacle which first kept him from becoming a Christian. Now, on his conversion it was thoroughly repudiated. We do not know what became of the concubine whom Augustine sent away, but from that time on, Augustine was never able to enjoy a conscience-free sexual relationship. His view of women and of sexual intercourse was never very positive after conversion.

He later connected sexual desire with a biological transmitter of 'original sin', the sin inherited after Adam and Eve's first disobedience. It was the parents' sexual lust which made every birth impure. For Augustine the starting point of Christianity thus became the fallen nature of humanity, the grace of God restoring that fall by means of Jesus' death on the cross, mediated through the sacraments. His views came to dominate later Catholic and Protestant thought, which will be contrasted below with the Eastern perspective of theosis and resurrection.

After his baptism Augustine decided to return from Italy to North Africa, where he was born. On the way, in Ostia, he shared an experience of union with God with his mother. They ascended in conversation until they in silence 'slightly touched' Wisdom.

Finally, after his mother's death, he returned to Africa, and because of his intellectual superiority was forcibly ordained a priest and later a bishop. In Hippo he established a monastic community around the cathedral, and entered a long career of writing and church administration.

In his conflict with **Pelagius** (c.354–after 418) Augustine championed the grace of God against human effort as the means of salvation. Pelagius, a contemporary of Augustine, experienced the weak-kneed mediocrity of Christians in Britain, his home, who gave up the moral battles of the Christian life by saying, 'I can't do it. If God wanted me to, God would give me the strength.' Relying on grace and not on human effort seemed a cop out to Pelagius.

This issue is fundamental to Christian spirituality, and was to be the prime reason for the later split in the church between Catholics and Protestants. How are we to understand the role of God as Saviour and the human being as actor in the Christian life? Augustine was convinced that any good thing in his life was a gift of God, not his own achievement. He had been rescued from his old life not by his own efforts, but by the love of God. If he had been able to save himself, there would have been no purpose in Jesus' death and resurrection.

In the long run, the Catholic Church sided with Augustine in its synod and council decisions, but in parishes the role of the human will in 'working out your salvation' was often more prominent. Later the Protestants would appeal to the anti-Pelagian writings to support their teaching of 'grace alone'.

Augustine also wrote treatises arguing against the Donatists, strict adherents of a purification movement among the Berber Christians to the south of his area. They were inheritors of the cult of martyrs, including Perpetua, and of the rigourist attitude of Tertullian. Augustine declared that baptisms performed by unworthy priests were still valid, whereas the Donatists accused clergy of deceiving the soldiers during persecution, and refused to receive their sacramental acts. Augustine became embroiled in a battle not only of words but of force, endorsing the use of soldiers against the Donatists. The split in the North African church was part of the reason that the church disappeared there after the Arab conquest in the seventh century.

In conclusion, Augustine left a mixed legacy for the Latin-speaking church. He was an intellectual who bound together the Platonist philosophical tradition with the biblical faith, emphasizing the Psalms and Paul. He was a synthesizer, who combined the basic insights of the Greek and Latin writers of the first four centuries into an orthodox vision of Truth. He was a sojourner who gave new expression to the personal walk from carnality to a loving God, with whom he sought union. He was a teacher whose bad conscience, unhealthy sexuality, and emphasis on original sin left a legacy of gloom and misogyny on much of Western spirituality. But for all his faults, Augustine's final word was adoration of the grace of God.

The second figure who stands at the roots of later Christian mysticism is an anonymous writer known to later centuries as **Dionysius the Areopagite**. It seems that a Syrian monk of about the year 500 wrote under the name of Dionysius in order to claim the authority which comes from the apostolic age, for nothing is known of the original Dionysius except his name in Acts 17:34. This writer is commonly known, therefore, as Pseudo-Dionysius. Four books have come down to us under this author's name: *The Celestial Hierarchy*, *The Ecclesiastical Hierarchy*, *The Divine Names*, and *Mystical Theology*.

Among his major contributions are the formulation of the three stages later to become standard in all Western mysticism, the purgative, illuminative and unitive. There were previous triads, but Pseudo-Dionysius was the first to name them in this way. 'Purgative' refers to a period of cleansing, 'illuminative' to the light of God shining on the soul, and 'unitive' to the experience of oneness with God.

The influence of Neo-Platonism, a later form of Plato's philosophy, is very strong in the conception of the spiritual life in 'Dionysius'. Much of his thought is parallel to that of Proclus, a contemporary non-Christian philosopher. Yet he has distinctly combined Christian understandings of God with the philosophical framework.

He operates with a world-view which is triadic and hierarchical—in fact he invented the word 'hierarchy' in Greek. Everything in the universe is seen to be in threes, with carefully described levels from top to bottom. He does not seem as interested in the relationship of Father, Son and Spirit as with the notion of threeness, which he sees at all levels of the hierarchy.

One of the most powerful and distinctive teachings of Dionysius is his apophatic theology, a theology beyond words and images. He begins his discussion of *The Divine Names* by echoing Paul in Romans 11 on the inscrutable nature of God.

Indeed the inscrutable One is out of the reach of every rational process. Nor can any words come up to the inexpressible Good, this One, this Source of all unity, this supra-existent Being. Mind beyond mind, word beyond speech, it is gathered up by no discourse, by no intuition, by no name.[29]

Then in *The Mystical Theology* Dionysius introduces the theme of divine darkness, of the need to strip away the intellect in the knowledge of God. He begins with poetry, which is a forerunner of St John of the Cross, whom we will meet in Chapter 5.

Trinity!! Higher than any being,
    any divinity, and goodness!
    Guide of Christians
    in the wisdom of heaven!
Lead us up beyond unknowing and light,
    up to the farthest, highest peak
    of mystic Scripture,
    where the mysteries of God's Word
    lie simple, absolute and unchangeable
    in the brilliant darkness of a hidden silence.
    Amid the deepest shadow
    they pour overwhelming light
    on what is most manifest.

> Amid the wholly unsensed and unseen
> they completely fill our sightless minds
> with treasures beyond all beauty.

> [Reader,]... leave behind you everything perceived and understood, everything perceptible and understandable, all that is not and all that is, and with your understanding laid aside, to strive upward as much as you can toward union with him who is beyond all being and knowledge. By an undivided and absolute abandonment of yourself and everything, shedding all and freed from all, you will be uplifted to the ray of the divine shadow which is above everything that is.[30]

He argued that since any human concept is inadequate for God, only denials of the likeness of God to human categories could properly apply. For example, it would limit God to say, 'God is just' (the positive way). But it would be better to say, 'God is not unjust' (the negative way). He asserts, however, after a long list of such negations, that God is even beyond denial.

The process of stripping one's concepts of God of all that is unworthy is called the *via negativa*, or the negative way. It is the intellectual side of apophatic theology. One of the striking features of the writings of 'Dionysius' is the combination of a highly intellectual discussion of God with an absolute denial of the power of the intellect to know God.

The affective side of apophatic spirituality is a state of utter passivity on the part of the mystic. According to 'Dionysius' such passivity leads to an ecstasy of love in which the human is fused with God. This theme is to be seen in a great deal of later mysticism, for example in Meister Eckhart, whom we will meet later (Chapter 4, below).

The opposite of apophatic is kataphatic, which means an active attempt to image God by the use of one's imagination and emotions. The practice of meditation by means of calling forth images from the Scriptures, for example, is kataphatic. 'Dionysius' clearly thinks that the kataphatic way has its utility, notably for beginners on the spiritual way. But for those approaching union, the apophatic way is necessary.

We conclude by noting again that Christianity in the early centuries developed in a number of cultures and was expressed somewhat differently in each of them. The foundational developments occurred not only in Greek and Latin contexts but in Syriac, Celtic and other contexts less well-known. The same themes we have discussed here—worship and sacraments, charisms, martyrdom, asceticism, monasticism and mysticism—appeared in

Ethiopia and Britain, India and Syria. It is clear, however, that the Greco-Roman synthesis was the dominant form in number and wealth.

Recommended Reading

Sebastian Brock, translator, *The Syriac Fathers on Prayer and the Spiritual Life*, Kalamazoo, Michigan: Cistercian, 1987.

Tito Colliander, *Way of the Ascetics: The Ancient Tradition of Discipline and Inner Growth*, St Vladimir's Seminary Press, 1989.

Esther de Waal, editor, *The Celtic Vision: Prayers and Blessings from the Outer Hebrides*, Darton, Longman and Todd, 1988.

Esther de Waal, *A World Made Whole*, London: Fount Paperbacks, 1991.

Ephrem the Syrian, *Hymns*, translated by Kathleen E. McVey, SCM Press, 1993. (*Classics of Western Spirituality* Series)

C.H. Lawrence, *Medieval Monasticism: Forms of Religious Life in Western Europe in the Middle Ages*, second edition, New York: Longman, 1989.

Noel Dermot O'Donoghue, ODC, *Aristocracy of Soul: Patrick of Ireland*, Wilmington: Michael Glazier, 1987.

Philip Sheldrake, *Living Between Worlds: Place and Journey in Celtic Spirituality*, Darton, Longman and Todd, 1995.

Patrick Thomas, *Candle in the Darkness: Celtic Spirituality from Wales*, Llandysul: Gomer Press, 1993.

The European Era

In this chapter, I will discuss Christian spirituality from about the seventh to the fifteenth centuries. I have called the chapter 'The European Era', because Christianity had lost ground geographically in Asia and Africa, but spread to new cultures in northern Europe, notably to the Anglo-Saxons, the Germans, the Scandinavians, the Ukrainians and the Russians. The development of spirituality in these new areas was to be significant for world history in centuries to follow.

It was a period of gradual separation of the Greek East from the Latin West. 'East' and 'West' here assume the Mediterranean Sea as the centre of the earth. The East centres now in Constantinople and the West in Rome. The usual date of separation of the Roman Catholic and Eastern Orthodox churches is 1054, but there were many ups and downs in this relationship from about 800 to 1200. The Fourth Crusade (1202) finally left bitterness beyond measure when Roman Catholics sacked the Eastern capital, Constantinople.

The East

In the early centuries, the differences between East and West were cultural, but the church had an overall unity of spirit, if no single leader or pope. The various ancient cities of the apostles, Jerusalem, Antioch, Ephesus, Alexandria, Rome, and later Constantinople, each had a patriarch. But the Patriarch of Rome, the only patriarch in the West, gradually claimed unique authority over the others. They did not agree to be ruled by him and tensions mounted.

Drawing on the traditions of Greek theology and the ecumenical councils up to 787, the Eastern church came to have distinctive emphases which differed from the West. The 'ecumenical' councils were those representing the whole 'inhabited world'. This is the same word used in the twentieth century for the movement to unify the churches of different denominations. The church was not divided into denominations at that time, so representatives from the Roman East and West participated at Nicea in 325, Constantinople in 381, Ephesus in 431, Chalcedon in 451, Constantinople (II) in 553, Constantinople (III) in 680–81, and Nicea (II) in 787. After this, the Roman Catholic Church continued to call councils, but they were not recognized by the Eastern Orthodox Church.

In the areas near the Mediterranean the Eastern church lived under Islamic rule after the seventh century, and was pressured to stop any evangelism or outward Christian display. In 1453 the unthinkable happened and the very centre of Byzantine rule fell to the Muslim Turks: the great cathedral Haggia Sophia became a mosque. No longer named Constantinople, the city has since been called Istanbul.

In the areas where missionaries had taken the new faith, notably the Ukraine and Russia, Christianity came to be associated with czars (caesars) as it had in Byzantine days, so Moscow counted itself the 'Third Rome', centre of a Christian empire after the fall of both Rome and Constantinople.

Eastern theology was strongly trinitarian, firmly based on the early councils, the Holy Tradition. It saw the spiritual development of the Christian in the schema of divinization or theosis, the process of humans becoming divine.

The Jesus Prayer was the prayer of the heart

The roots of the Jesus Prayer lie in Scripture. The publican prayed, 'God, be merciful to me, a sinner!';[1] Paul exhorted, 'Pray without ceasing';[2] and Peter preached, 'This man is standing before you in good health by the name of Jesus Christ of Nazareth... There is no other name under heaven given among mortals by which we must be saved.'[3] The fundamental idea of the Jesus Prayer is to pray constantly. This requires a kind of attention to God which becomes habitual while one goes about the tasks of daily life. The prayer is a short formula which is repeated constantly, in rhythm with one's breathing or heartbeat. After a period of learning, the prayer repeats itself naturally without conscious effort. It is sometimes called 'the prayer of the heart'.

Today the most common form of the prayer is 'Lord Jesus Christ, have mercy on me.' But the emergence of the prayer was gradual. Different forms of words and different understandings of their function can be seen in the fifth to eighth centuries. Kallistos Ware, a present-day scholar and bishop of the Orthodox Church writes that there were four elements which eventually came together in this prayer:

1. Devotion to the Holy Name 'Jesus', which is felt to act in a semi-sacramental way as a source of power and grace.
2. The appeal for divine mercy, accompanied by a keen sense of compunction and inward grief (*penthos*).
3. The discipline of frequent repetition.
4. The quest for inner silence or stillness (*hesuchia*), that is to say, for imageless, non-discursive prayer.[4]

Some elements of the prayer can be found in the desert fathers and mothers, but it develops distinctively later with Diadochus (fifth century), who was influenced by Evagrius in seeking 'prayer without thoughts', that is without images or words, but gave a practical method for seeking it (see point 4 above). But he was also influenced by Macarius in an affective emphasis, valuing experience and not just intellect.

It may be surprising for us today that the Jesus Prayer was further developed in Gaza and Sinai, areas of recent Middle East conflict, by monks with names such as Barsanuphius, John, Dorotheus, Philemon, John Climacus, Hesychius and Philotheus. The Sinai writers may hint at the connection between the recitation of the prayer and the rhythm of breathing, which became explicit in the Middle Ages.

It was in the Middle Ages that the prayer became widely used among Orthodox monks. Much later, in the late nineteenth century, the anonymous *Way of a Pilgrim* took the prayer to the West from Russia. Ware says that it is used in the twentieth century by more Christians, East and West, than in any century before. He clarifies its practice by writing,

> By modern Western writers it is sometimes termed a 'Christian mantra', but this could give rise to confusion. The Jesus Prayer is not simply a rhythmic incantation, but an invocation addressed directly to the person of Jesus Christ, and it presupposes conscious, active faith in him as only-begotten Son of God and unique Saviour. It is not,

however, a form of discursive meditation upon particular incidents in Christ's life, but has as its aim to bring us to the level of *hesuchia* or stillness—to a state of intuitive, non-discursive awareness in which we no longer form pictures in our mind's eye or analyse concepts with our reasoning brain, but feel and know the Lord's immediate presence in a direct personal encounter.[5]

From this apophatic practice we turn to one which is also distinctively Eastern, but emphatically kataphatic: the use of icons in worship. The apophatic moves beyond images; the kataphatic employs images.

Icons were windows to heaven

The visual representation of the human form in a certain style came to be a distinctive spiritual and theological expression of Orthodox Christianity. Icons, it is claimed by the Orthodox, were present even in the time of the apostles, and were an intrinsic part of the Christian message from the beginning. We might expect, however, that only after the time of Constantine, when the churches had a stable existence, large buildings and financial resources, did the golden paintings we know today begin to emerge.

The status of icons was clarified in the eighth and ninth centuries during the Iconoclastic Controversies. These were theological and political disputes within Eastern Orthodoxy. The major theological issue behind the conflict was the nature of the incarnation. Did the Word of God really become flesh, really enter the material world in Jesus of Nazareth? If so, as the doctrinal tradition claimed, then what were the implications for the nature of Christian worship? Was the adoration of God to be purely mental, or did images and human art have an important role to play?

Iconoclasts, those who wanted to throw the paintings out of the church, argued that it was unworthy of God to be represented and venerated in a physical object. The veneration of paintings and statues appeared as idolatry from this point of view. Some of the emperors in Constantinople used their power to physically destroy icons. (Compare this view to that of the Puritan Cromwell in the English Civil War of the 1640s. His followers destroyed many statues and paintings.)

Defenders of such representation and veneration replied that this practice was consistent with the mystery of the incarnation. It was taking seriously the human nature of Jesus, the goodness of creation, and the sacramental quality of all things, for it implied that a physical object could be the meeting place between God and human beings.

The seventh ecumenical council in 787 approved the use of icons stating, 'The honor rendered to the image passes to its prototype, and the person who venerates an icon venerates the person (*hypostasis*) represented in it.'[6]

Thus one of the most distinctive features of all Eastern Orthodox Christianity was preserved. Today as then, the human figures in the icons are seen as windows on eternity, as means by which worshippers may participate in the divine. Eastern Orthodox spirituality continues a devotion to Jesus, his mother the 'Theotokos' or Bearer of God, and all the saints, by means of lighting candles and incense before icons and kissing them. Family and private worship also include this practice, for many Orthodox homes have a special place of worship with icons.

In our time worship with icons could be called 'right brain' prayer, using images rather than discursive language. It is one kataphatic approach in the Eastern tradition, along with elaborate liturgical gestures and architectural symbolism in churches. The apophatic approach is also present in the East, as seen for example in the Jesus Prayer. These need not exclude each other, but both can be practised to complement each other.

Gregory Palamas defended hesychasm at Mount Athos

Hesychia (or *hesuchia*), stillness or silence, is the word for a prime tradition in Eastern spirituality. It refers to going apart to the desert for solitude. Its greatest theologian and defender was **Gregory Palamas** (1296–1359), a monk of the famous group of monasteries at Athos in Greece, archbishop of Thessalonika, and writer of many theological volumes.

Typical of the Eastern tradition, Gregory saw the goal of the Christian life in the statement of Athanasius, 'God became man so that man might become God.'[7] This implies that the major axis of the faith is not human sin and divine redemption on the cross, but rather human mortality and divine victory in the resurrection. The incarnation of God in Jesus was the way in which God defeated the powers of death and sin through the passion, death and resurrection of Jesus.

Gregory and the other monks on Athos, experiencing a spiritual revival there, were attacked by an Eastern theologian of Western training, named Barlaam. It is he who caused Gregory to break his silence and defend in his writings many of the distinctive characteristics of Eastern spirituality. Notably, he approved of trying new methods, even if some should later be found wanting, in seeking union with God, which is the process of divinization.

As a theologian, Gregory made the important distinction between the energies of God, which humans may know, and the essence of God, which they cannot know. He defended the possibility of a vision of God in this life, even before death, though it is not perfect. He defended various extreme physical disciplines used with the Jesus Prayer. Thus Palamas disagreed with Barlaam, urging the importance of the body and its postures in prayer.

He stated that union with God is essentially by God's grace, yet the vision of God in this life could not be attained without hard work, and was easier for solitary monks than for the married. There is a cooperation or *synergy* between the divine grace and human will: Whoever searches with all their hearts for unceasing prayer will be given the gift of prayer (a gift of grace). The gift of tears (a constant flow of joyful tears) will be given to those whose passion for things of earth is being transformed into passion for things of heaven. Unlike some earlier writers, Gregory sees positive passions as well as negative ones. Thus for him 'passionlessness' (*apatheia*), or freedom from destructive passions, does not refer to a denial of the body, but the transformation of body and soul together.

For Gregory Palamas, the transfiguration of Jesus was the revelatory event which showed the present and future kingdom of God. The glory of God and of Christ was visible to the three disciples as a sign of the actual presence of the kingdom. That kingdom is still present for those given the gift of seeing it, but it will be perfected for those who after death see God face to face.

The West

As the East in this period was characterized by icons, the Jesus Prayer, and hesychasm, in the context of a monastic church spreading northward, the West also spread north, developing new forms of religious orders and mysticism. Western Europe focused more on sin as the enemy of humankind and the cross of Jesus as its solution, as compared with the Eastern focus on death as the enemy and the resurrection of the Christ as the victory of God.

Monasticism was renewed by spiritual leaders

Among the great medieval spiritual teachers is **Anselm of Canterbury** (1033–1109). He is known for his contributions to systematic theology (his teaching of atonement by satisfaction of God's justice) and to philosophical theology (his ontological argument for the existence of God). His life of deep piety produced these writings which became a bridge between the early writers and the Middle Ages. His theme phrase came originally from Augustine: 'I believe so that I may understand, and what is more I believe that unless I do believe, I shall not understand.'[8]

Anselm wrote *Prayers and Meditations* to help others pray. It shows his commitment to thoughtful meditation, the combination of rigorous intellectual work and devotion to God in Christ.

Within the Western tradition, no one was greater in the twelfth century than **Bernard of Clairvaux** (1090–1153). He was known for reform of the monastic tradition, returning to the simplicity of the *Rule* of St Benedict, and eventually administering a vast network of monasteries. In his public life he preached to recruit participants in the Second Crusade in 1146, and in later life had so much power he was the virtual pope of the Western church. Our brief survey cannot recount the story of this dramatic and troubled series of events.

Bernard was declared a doctor of the Roman Catholic Church by Pope Pius XII in 1953. The encyclical declaring this honour is called *Doctor Mellifluus* (or the doctor-flowing-with-honey) because of the sweetness of his teaching compared with the dryness or harshness of some other medieval writers. Indeed his teaching, focusing as it does on love, is both positive and personal but not sentimental, as the title may suggest.[9]

In his teaching on the spiritual life, Bernard focuses most clearly on the relationship between the self and God. Borrowing a good deal from Augustine, Bernard, in his treatise 'On Loving God', sets forth four degrees of this love. He sees the self first of all loving only itself, then loving the neighbour and God for its own sake. Thirdly the soul comes to love God for God's sake, normally the highest plane of love. But there is a fourth level, in which the soul loves itself for God's sake. This is found only fleetingly on earth, but will be the constant state of the dead after the resurrection of the body.[10]

Bernard emphasizes the importance of the human Jesus for Christian spirituality. He refers more frequently than his immediate predecessors to the New Testament portrait of Jesus not merely as an example of a holy life, but as the divine action of love to change the hearts of human beings. Bernard's sermons on Advent and Christmas rise to the heights of praise for the incarnation.

His *Sermons on the Song of Songs* are a striking example of 'spiritual' interpretation of the Bible. The eighty-six discourses cover only the first two chapters of the Song, but the most striking feature to a modern reader is the breathtaking reversal of the sensuous, erotic metaphors of the poems to an appeal against the passions of the flesh, and a description of the joys of spiritual intimacy with God. Here the Bridegroom is Jesus and the Bride, the soul of the Christian.

> What a close and intimate relation this grace produces between the Divine Word and the soul, and what confidence follows from that intimacy, you may well imagine. I believe that a soul in such condition may say without fear, 'My Beloved is mine...'[11]

Writers in our time have suggested that the roles be reversed, and that God or Jesus become the female partner. The passionate nature of God's love is emphasized here, suggesting a divine *eros* for humanity, in contrast to the dispassionate *agape* as it has been interpreted by some Protestant writers.[12] Eros suggests the kind of longing experienced by lovers, whereas agape has been portrayed as the love of the unlovable, a determination of the will to seek what is good for the one loved. Both words are needed, in my opinion, to convey the richness of God's love.

Bernard emphasized the role of humility in the Christian life, for example in his comments on the Song of Songs. The knowledge essential for the Christian is knowledge of the self and of God. Such self-knowledge is humility. He says, 'There is no danger, however much you may humble yourself, that you will regard yourself as much less than you really are—that is to say, than truth holds you to be.'[13]

In the light of modern psychology, many of us would demur at this point, and argue that a healthy regard for one's worth before God can enhance rather than retard the loving relationship. Or, to put it another way, Bernard has looked at one particular danger to the relationship with God, that of arrogant pride, but he has not seen the opposite danger—such a low self-regard that the soul cannot enter a relationship with the divine. This too might be a perverse form of pride.

A movement to revive the ideals of twelfth-century monasticism was begun by Gerard Groote in late fourteenth-century Netherlands. It came to be called the 'modern devotion' not really because it was something new but because it sought to develop a devotion to Christ which was as characteristic of life outside the cloister as within it. The movement developed into a monastic order, a subgroup of the Augustinians called the Windesheim Congregation, but also to a group of over one hundred houses in Holland and Germany of the Sisters of the Common Life and the Brothers of the Common Life. These disturbed some people because they had all the appearances of a new monastic order but without permission. The members practised poverty, celibacy and obedience, but never took formal vows. Their daily life was very much like that of the Benedictines.

What was distinctive in the Sisters and the Brothers was a spirituality which focused on the imitation of Christ. This theme, which became the title of the best known book of spirituality throughout western Europe, demanded that disciples of Jesus follow the way of the cross. Knowledge of the self and denial of the self, together with contempt for the world are enjoined on the reader. The probable author is **Thomas à Kempis** (1380–1471), one of half a dozen major leaders in this movement. The book breathes a strong eucharistic piety as well as the practice of constant meditation, not only during quiet times, but in the midst of work.

The 'Modern Devotion' differs from the best of twelfth-century spirituality by seeing no value in the intellectual life. The intricacies of scholasticism and the immoral lives of some monks who claimed to be learned had convinced its members that true knowledge does not come from books but from the identification of one's life with God, the fusion of knower and known. One of the famous paragraphs in *The Imitation of Christ* reads:

> What good does it do to speak learnedly about the Trinity if lacking
> humility you displease the Trinity? Indeed it is not learning that makes
> man holy and just, but a virtuous life makes him pleasing to God. I
> would rather feel contrition than know how to define it. What would
> it profit us to know the whole Bible by heart and the principles of all

the philosophers if we live without grace and the love of God? Vanity of vanities, all is vanity except to have God and serve him alone.[14]

This view was to influence Protestant pietism in later centuries. It is a good reminder that theology calls for an appropriate life as well as intellectual tools; spirituality is part of theology. But it can also lead to despising one of God's good gifts, the human intellect.

Mendicant orders emerged as a new form of religious life

The thirteenth century was a time of important developments for Christian spirituality and theology. It is commonly regarded as the peak of the 'high' Middle Ages, that is, the time of fruition and fullest development in this period of history.

Among the dramatic events was the founding of mendicant (begging) orders, a new development in the history of monasticism. The Dominicans, the Franciscans, the Carmelites and the Augustinians exemplified a new understanding of the need to meet the needs of the church and the society. Instead of binding themselves to stay in one monastery, there to engage in communal and private prayer, these new orders called for service in the world as the first priority. To varying degrees they retained 'monasteries' (now 'houses'), common prayer and direction by an 'abbot' (now a 'prior'). All continued the basic vows of poverty, chastity and obedience, but the practice of these vows was adapted to new circumstances.

Dominic Guzman (about 1170–1221) saw the need for better preaching in the Catholic Church. Heretics in southern France were making inroads on an uneducated laity; the typical and damaging response of rulers was to put the heretics down by military might. Dominic had experienced some success in persuasion rather than force. He founded an order of preachers, commonly called Dominicans, who could speak to the people with knowledge and effectiveness. Very soon this order became one of the best educated groups in Europe, and its spirituality focused on the piety of learning.

Studying and preaching came to have even more value for this order than poverty or obedience. Mendicancy (begging for one's living) was eventually abandoned as impractical, and obedience was in tension with the understanding that the preacher is independent and that the rule of the order was a human instrument, not a divine law. The order retained a great deal of flexibility, and developed one of the most adaptable systems of governance, which was later copied by many subsequent orders.

It helped produce some of the greatest scholars in the history of Europe, namely **Albert the Great** (about 1200–80) and his student **Thomas Aquinas** (1225–74). Thomas was later the most influential theologian in the Catholic Church, having incorporated the philosophical perspectives of Aristotle into the theological tradition he inherited from Augustine and many others.

Thomas viewed the Christian life as a colloquy or friendship between humans and God, emphasizing the role of charity as the measure of all vows, practices and steps. It is said that Thomas himself left the work on his great work, the *Summa Theologica*, for the sake of a life of prayer and meditation. All he had written was but as straw compared with the wonders he experienced in a mystical unity with God.

It was another Dominican, Alan de La Roche, who in the late fifteenth century introduced one of the most popular and enduring features of Catholic piety: the rosary. The rosary is a physical aid to prayer and meditation, consisting of 150 beads, usually formed into a circle with a crucifix attached. Praying the rosary is a way of both repeating familiar prayers (the Our Father, the Hail Mary, and the Doxology) and meditating on sacred 'mysteries', that is, important events in the lives of Mary and Jesus. There are five Joyful Mysteries relating to the birth of Jesus, five Sorrowful Mysteries concerning the suffering of Jesus, and five Glorious Mysteries, recounting the resurrection of Jesus and the honouring of Mary. These fifteen mysteries are recalled in concert with the 150 beads.

Thus the mind operates on two levels: the repetition is simply a way of centring the attention, while the mysteries are imaginatively relived. Obviously this devotion depends on the belief that Mary, together with all the saints, is able to hear the prayers of the faithful, and is an appropriate mediator to her son Jesus and to God. Most Protestants have not been willing to accept these beliefs, but a few in our own day are advocating the use of the rosary by Protestants. Roman Catholics have made the rosary less prominent since the Second Vatican Council, especially in public worship.

The second great founder of a mendicant order, and surely one of the most fascinating and challenging figures of the whole medieval period is **Francis of Assisi** (1181/2–1226), founder of the Franciscan Order or the

'Friars Minor' (little brothers). His life is associated also with **Clare of Assisi** (1193–1253), the founder of the 'Second Order' for women or the 'Poor Clares'. It is difficult to write briefly about figures whose lives have attracted so much attention, so many legends, so many analyses.

Francis has been called the saint who most clearly exemplifies the life of his Saviour, with whose love he was enflamed. It began when a young, enthusiastic, worldly youth heard the call of the gospel passage in which Jesus sent out his disciples to preach in Galilee. Francis was given love for lepers and the desire to 'rebuild' the church. He fell in love with 'Lady Poverty' and wandered as a mendicant, praying, preaching, helping. He found freedom from possessions so exhilarating, that he determined to own nothing of his own. Soon others were attracted by his joy and simplicity, and the band of twelve were approved as the Order of Friars Minor.

Later Francis was forced to compose a Rule for the rapidly expanding order. He was never known as a gifted administrator, but rather as a free spirit. He visited the Holy Land and preached to the Muslim Saracens, and in 1224 retired to pray on Mount La Verna. There he received the answer to his prayer for identification with the Saviour: the *stigmata* of Christ, the wounds of the crucified Jesus appeared in Francis' flesh.

It was after this, in his last two years of life, that he wrote his well-known *Canticle to the Sun*, in which he addresses all things in creation as his brothers and sisters. Even death in this poem becomes a sibling of the singer, in a sharp reversal of the attitude of Paul and others who saw death as an enemy.

Francis, writing about the sun and moon, the fire and air, as siblings, is one of the few outstanding spiritual writers to make the fourth relationship of our model, the relation to the creation, a major part of his message. The legends of Francis and the wolf and Francis preaching to the birds extend his simple theme of the Fatherhood of God to all creatures, not just to humans. The humility and the joy expressed in this man encompass both identification with the pains of the crucified Jesus and the happy and carefree humility which trusted the Father of birds and flowers to provide his needs.

Clare, a woman of Assisi who had observed Francis for some time, asked to become a member of his band. She became the leader of the Second Order for women, whose life was more traditionally monastic; the sisters did not wander from place to place as the men did. For her, poverty was the door to contemplation of the Jesus who was himself poor and served the poor.

A Third (Franciscan) Order for lay people was added later, and became a powerful stimulant to Christian life for those not called to the life of the religious orders.

The men's order developed with much internal strife after the initial bands had expanded and the influence of the magnetic personality of Francis no longer personally influenced the new members. Greater or lesser strictness concerning poverty was the debating point for centuries to come.

One of the greatest Franciscans was **St Bonaventure** (1217–74), who was minister general of the order. He integrated his great learning of the classics with the influence of Francis in a large number of writings.

Mysticism came to a new flowering

Women and men who gave themselves to a life of prayer and meditation in the late Middle Ages are commonly called mystics. At times mysticism became faddish, and there was a great deal of phony pretension and seeking after supernatural phenomena. The best mystics always warned against seeking flashy effects in favour of seeking God alone.

One can distinguish two basic kinds of mystics, those who were more affective (focused on the affections) and those who were more intellectual and philosophical. The former type included many whose writings have been called 'Bride-mysticism' because of concentration on the images from Song of Songs relating to marriage to Christ the Bridegroom. Bernard of Clairvaux fits this description.

Of the latter type, the most outstanding example is **Meister Eckhart** (1260?–1328?), a Dominican who influenced John Tauler (1300?–61) and many other influential preachers and writers. His vague expressions in his German sermons led to considerable confusion as to his exact meaning. Near the end of his life some of his Franciscan enemies brought charges against him, and a number of his statements were condemned as heretical. He was accused of heresies related to Neo-Platonism: pantheism (the view that God is the world and the world is God), making no distinction between God and the soul in mystical union, and the denial of God's freedom in creation. The validity of these condemnations is still hotly debated by the adherents of 'creation spirituality' (see Chapter 7). They contend that Eckhart was a biblical preacher. He was influenced by Celtic and Eastern Christianity, and served communities of women called Beguines. These women were not wealthy enough to have a dowry for entrance into a monastery, so lived their according to their own rule in the world. The Beguin movement began in 1223 in the Rhine valley, but was condemned about a century later by Pope John XXII.[40] Eckhart was influenced by these women, and especially by Mechthild of Magdeburg.

An important issue is how much Eckhart is to be seen as a Neo-Platonist author and how much as a biblical one. It seems that Pseudo-Dionysius was a very strong influence, especially on Eckhart's doctrine of God.

There are many women and men who could be chosen for discussion in this section. Among them are Hildegard of Bingen (1109–79), an abbess on the Rhine who included visual art in the reports of her visions; Joachim of Fiore (about 1135–1202) who developed a distinctive apocalyptic spirituality; Henry Suso (about 1295–1366), another Dominican follower of Eckhart; Catherine of Sienna (about 1347–80), whose concern for reform of the church led to direct influence on the pope; Catherine of Genoa (1447–1510), called the 'Theologian of Purgatory'; and Walter Hilton (d. 1396), Richard Rolle (about 1300–49), and the unknown author of *The Cloud of Unknowing*, all English mystics of the fourteenth century.

I have chosen two mystics for closer attention, Jan van Ruysbroeck and Julian of Norwich. The first of these, **Jan van Ruysbroeck** (1293–1381), though not widely known, is highly regarded by students of mysticism because he drew together the two major strands of mysticism, the affective and the intellectual. He shows the influence of Pseudo-Dionysius, Augustine, Bernard of Clairvaux and Meister Eckhart. After serving for twenty-six years as a secular priest, Jan and three other mystics withdrew to a forest priory near Brussels. He composed his major works there in vernacular Flemish.

In *The Spiritual Espousals* Ruysbroeck uses and modifies the traditional three-stage schema of mystical growth: (a) the purgative, (b) the illuminative and (c) the unitive. The most important change is his repeated insistence that the stages do not follow one after the other, but are added on. Thus the first is included in the second, the first and second in the third. These three differ from the traditional arrangement also by including true union with God already in the second stage, though intermittently.

Ruysbroeck calls his stages (a) the active life, (b) the interior or yearning life, and (c) the God-seeing or contemplative life. In *The Sparkling Stone* wayfarers on these steps are named respectively the faithful servants, the secret friends and the hidden sons of God.

(a) The spiritual life begins with conversion. The person uses free will to turn to God and begin the way back to God. Such a turning is empowered by grace and results in charity. This turning then leads to the cleansing of conscience through contrition, penance and dislike of oneself. One is truly in the active life when by means of the light of grace, a will turned to God and a clean conscience, the spiritual eyes are opened. One enters a life of virtue and service to others.

(b) To this life of exterior works the second stage adds the practice of interior exercises. It is in this stage that the imagination must be purged of all creaturely images, all clinging to the world, that the soul may be prepared for God. Whereas in the first stage, one's union with God was achieved through grace and works and sacraments, in the second stage one begins to know union with God without such means.

(c) In the third stage, the union with God which the yearner has known in the second stage becomes of a higher and more permanent quality. Whereas the person was characterized by a seeking and a great hunger, he or she is now at rest, in 'fruition' or 'delectation'. Yet one who has attained this 'fruition' lives an active life also. This highest life Ruysbroeck calls 'common'. It is life in both contemplation and service, given to all people in common as God gives to all in common.

These stages of union with God, are accompanied by a unification of the self as well. Likewise, though to a lesser degree, the wayfarer is united to other people. Using one of his favourite metaphors, fluid, Ruysbroeck explains how one is melted by the heat of the Holy Spirit, and flows out to all types of persons.

Holiness in unity means the discarding of multiplicity, or at least all things opposed to one's union with the One. Intellectually, this means approaching God with a bare mind, aware that 'desire and love go in where understanding is not admitted'.[15] It means entering the divine darkness, having removed creaturely images from the mind.

Volitionally it means abandoning one's will to God's will. This involves aligning all one's affections Godward, not clinging to anything in the world. And finally it means dying to oneself, 'melting' and flowing into God. Whereas the 'friends of God' (those in stage (b)) 'keep something of their own selfhood, and are not consumed and burned to nothing in the unity of love', 'the sons [in stage (c)] experience a simple and deathlike passing which is in no wise'.[16] In the highest stage the spirit feels itself dead and lost to itself, and one with God without difference and without distinction... And this is an unfathomable abyss wherein man must die to himself in blessedness, and must live again in virtues, whenever love and its stirring demand it.[17]

Ruysbroeck, like many other mystics, is not always easy to read. Although his work is clearly organized, he warns the reader, 'And observe with diligence and care, for whoever has not felt this shall not easily understand it.'[18]

In spite of his many words, Ruysbroeck usually has a light and joyful tone. He is far from morbid, always pointing to joy, peace, rest and enjoyment in God. Though he indicates an awareness of sin, it remains on the periphery of his vision; he focuses on God and the blessings of union with God.

Ruysbroeck instructs the reader in an objective tone, never directly speaking of himself. He will speak of 'man' even when it seems he is indirectly referring to his own experience. His description of 'spiritual drunkenness', which must reflect some of his own experience, is one of the most memorable paragraphs in the Spiritual Espousals. His basic approach is not to say 'this is what I have seen' as does Julian of Norwich (see below), but rather 'this is what may be seen'. He maps the terrain of the spirit, which includes highly subjective features, in an objective tone.

As we look at Ruysbroeck's writings we see a focus on the relationship between the self and God as primary, with some attention to the self's relation to itself and to others. Union with God is the dominant theme, unification of the self is corollary. The relationship to creation seems to be a negative one. According to Ruysbroeck, the world even in the positive sense of creation is a hindrance to union with God and plays no positive role in Christian spirituality.

Julian of Norwich (1353–1416?), for long centuries unknown, has come into prominence in the late twentieth century. Most of what we know about her is from a single book in two versions, a Short Text and a Long Text, commonly known as Revelations of Divine Love. She tells us that when she was thirty and a half years old she not only was on the point of death, but she received an answer to prayer that she should share in the sufferings of Christ on the cross. In fact, she was given sixteen visions or 'showings' which far exceeded the extent of her prayer. They were recorded soon afterwards in the Short Text.

She spent the next twenty years pondering and praying over these showings, as the Long Text indicates. In the meantime she had become an anchoress, a woman who lived a solitary life in a small cell attached to the church of St Julian in Norwich. So little do we know of biographical detail, that we do not know her name, but only the name of the church which we use to identify her.

Julian's writing was informed by knowledge of Paul's letters and the Gospel of John. She also knew the main ideas of Augustine, yet she regarded herself as unlettered. Perhaps she did not know Latin, but this, the first book in English known to be written by a woman, shows remarkable learning.

It is easy to contrast Julian's writing with that of her contemporary Margery Kempe, whose autobiography tells how she went to consult Julian. Margery's spiritual life was characterized by copious tears, loud groans and erotic images, which made most of her male acquaintances very uneasy! Margery writes that she found her visit with Julian comforting and reassuring, which does not surprise the reader of Julian's book.

Julian is also known for writing of Jesus as our Mother. She did not invent the image, since other spiritual writers had drawn upon it before her. But she uses it in a more theologically knowledgeable way than her predecessors. It is not just that mother love is an illustration of Jesus' love for us, she says, but the very nature of his relation to us is explained by it.[19]

In contrast to Ruysbroeck, Julian is not interested in mapping out the mystical landscape, in discussing the stages of the way, or even in giving rules for the moral life. Rather, she is setting out carefully, intellectually, the conclusions of years of pondering her showings. She is more interested in inquiring into the mysteries of God, humanity, sin and redemption, than in charting her own spiritual progress or that of others. Thus she is recognized today as a theologian, not simply a visionary.

Julian's dominating question is how to understand the presence of sin in a world created good by a good creator. She does not answer the question in discursive theology, but by pondering the images and narrative of one of her showings. In this showing, a lord sends his servant on an important errand, but the servant falls into a pit. The master looks on him 'with pity not with blame'. This fall is taken to be both the fall of Adam into sin and the self-emptying of Christ in becoming human. In the end, Julian says, sin was 'behovely' or necessary for the fulness of God's plan to send Christ and to rouse humanity to love. She concludes with a beautiful passage showing that the underlying theme of the whole is the love of God.

And from the time that it was revealed, I desired many times to know in what was our Lord's meaning. And fifteen years after and more, I was answered in spiritual understanding, and it was said: What, do you wish to know your Lord's meaning in this thing? Know it well, love was his meaning. Who reveals it to you? Love. What did he reveal to you? Love. Why does he reveal it to you? For love.[20]

There is an eschatological dimension in Julian's vision which is often lacking in mystical writers. That is, she looks forward to the consummation of all things. The world may be as a small hazelnut in a human hand, but it is precious to God, and God will redeem it. We do not get the sense in Julian that the world is only a shell, to be thrown away like rubbish for the sake of human souls, but that just as Paul writes in Romans 8, the creation will share in the redemption of the children of God. Her statement quoted and made famous by T.S. Eliot is 'All shall be well, and all manner of things shall be well.' Notice that she does not gloss over the reality of sin and evil. Fourteenth-century Norwich was a place that knew war, plague and famine. No, it is rather that she looks forward to a mysterious act of God which she does not attempt to explain, by which God's love will triumph over the very real sin and evil present in God's creation.

Because of her interest in the theological problems associated with evil in the world and her hope for a changed creation, Julian has among the most balanced views when considered by the four dimensions of spirituality discussed in this book.

Recommended Reading

Simon Barrington-Ward, *The Jesus Prayer*, Bible Reading Fellowship, 1996.

Grace M. Jantzen, *Julian of Norwich: Mystic and Theologian*, SPCK, 1992.

Julian of Norwich, *Revelations of Divine Love*, translated by James Walsh, SJ, A. Clarke Books, n.d.

Jean Leclerq, OSB, *The Love of Learning and the Desire for God: A Study of Monastic Culture*, Fordham University Press, 1993.

John Meyendorff, *Byzantine Theology: Historical Trends and Doctrinal Themes*, New York: Fordham University Press, 1993.

John Ruusbroec,* *John Ruusbroec: The Spiritual Espousals and Other Works*, translated by James A. Wiseman, OSB, SCM Press, 1993. (*Classics of Western Spirituality* Series)

* This is simply another spelling for Jan van Ruysbroeck.

Protestant and Catholic Reform

The sixteenth century was a time of religious turmoil even greater than earlier centuries. Northern Europe broke away from the South and East in a wrenching struggle which was to divide Europe for 400 years and more. Most thoughtful Catholics agreed that reform was needed, but there were very different views about it. Those Catholics who became Protestant came to the view that not only church political structures needed reform, but theology, liturgy, sacraments and spirituality did too. Separation from the papacy was the inevitable result.

Reformers who remained Catholic, on the other hand, managed to get approval at the Council of Trent for educational reform for priests, correction of obvious abuses by the bishops, and a more centralized administration of the church. The Catholics of Spain led the way in spiritual reform.

Both sides would transform Western Christendom, making a clear break from the later Middle Ages into the modern era.

The Protestant Reformation reshaped Christian spirituality

Luther and Lutherans emphasized grace and freedom

It was a spiritual problem which drove **Martin Luther** (1483–1546) to the extraordinary lengths of leading a Reformation. His search for a gracious

God amidst the many religious duties of late medieval piety could not satisfy him. Only when he understood Paul's words about the gospel and the righteousness of God in Romans 1 did the gates of paradise open. He understood for the first time that God's righteousness was a free gift, not a human achievement. He felt that he had been set free from the law of penances, pilgrimages, and monasteries, in order to love his neighbour in the ordinary deeds of daily life.

Unlike some other reformers, Luther did not want to abandon the Catholic heritage but to reform it. His norm was his understanding of the gospel, that people are justified by grace through faith. By this yardstick he decided to keep most of the mass, vestments, calendar and architecture of the church.

But he introduced the vernacular Bible, hymn singing and reform of the confessional; he oversaw the end of churchly pilgrimages (visiting distant holy places), relics (supposed bones and artifacts related to biblical figures and saints), and vows of celibacy (no sex). These he saw as human attempts to merit what could never be merited, but only received—the grace of God.

Just as we look back on the tradition today to decide what is helpful and what is not, so Luther did in his time. As he looked back on the writings of the fathers and the mystics, he used the gospel articulated by Paul as the standard by which he judged the spiritual tradition. This led him to approve some writers and disapprove of others.[1]

He loved to quote Augustine's anti-Pelagian writings and Bernard on the passive role of the soul before God. But he was not friendly to that stream of mysticism from Pseudo-Dionysius which became very philosophical in the hands of Meister Eckhart. Just as Luther came to see Aristotle as the great enemy in theology, so also in spirituality he opposed the foreign influence of Greek philosophy.

Luther's appreciation of the mystical tradition can be seen in his publication of the *Theologica Germanica*, an anonymous treatise from the previous century. Twice he saw this book through the press because he thought it helpful to the lay reader. His own more distinctive perspectives, however, come out in *The Freedom of a Christian* (1520). The mystical image of the marriage of the soul to Christ here takes on a new significance: the exchange of Christ's righteousness for the soul's sin. The treatise begins with paradoxical statements, a feature of Luther's thought on many subjects: 'The Christian is a perfectly free lord of all, subject to none. The Christian is a slave of all, subject to all.'[2]

At the root of this paradox is his view that the gospel has set us free from sin, death and Satan, but the gospel also sets us free to serve our neighbours, as we become Christs to them.

Luther struggled with *Anfechtungen* or spiritual attacks all his life. Anfechtung meant deep despair, a challenge to his standing before God, falling into an abyss of guilt and the taunts of Satan. Luther did not view these experiences as inevitable parts of the spiritual journey, but as spiritual warfare with evil. The objective, sacramental side of his faith came to his rescue here, for he could answer, 'I am baptized', and thus still his doubts, for he believed God had laid claim to him, however weak or sinful he might be.

In fact, Luther believed that Christians remain sinners all their lives. For all their good intentions and good works, all their prayers and Bible reading, they remained sinners, and their pious sins were sometimes worse than those of the flesh. He claimed that Christians are simultaneously saints and sinners; both condemned under the perfect law of God, and at the same time regarded by God as perfectly righteous because of the atonement of Jesus on the cross. Thus he did not expect very much external change in Christian growth; he was suspicious of claims to growth in holiness, and did not count such growth as his goal. Luther simply wanted to remain faithful to the cross as a sinner; no movement beyond that point seemed safe.

Luther's teaching on spirituality was very pragmatic, yet suspicious of methods to attain union with God. When asked by his barber how to pray, Luther replied with a very practical letter. In it he advises returning to the basics: the Ten Commandments, the Creed, and the Lord's Prayer. Make a garland, he advised, by finding in each part of these teachings something to learn, something for which to ask forgiveness, something to praise and thank God for, and a petition for aid of someone.[3]

This same return to the basics surely underlies Luther's *Small Catechism* which has affected the spirituality of Lutherans ever since. In it Luther explains these same basic documents in a way parallel to Jesus' Sermon on the Mount, where he internalized the old commands of Israel, allowing no one to claim innocence.

Luther called for a 'spirituality of the cross' as well as a 'theology of the cross'. The 'theology of glory', which he opposed, stood outside the human condition to interpret everything as a great system, much as Aristotle had done and the medieval theologians were doing. Luther's 'theology of the cross', however, began with the suffering of Christ on the cross which went against human reason and expectation. Here on the cross one finds God, Luther said. Here God is crucified and reveals his loving grace to humankind. A spirituality of the cross likewise is a following of Jesus through suffering and pain, not a triumphal vicarious thrill which elevates one to the heavens.

Luther's spirituality was focused on the freedom he experienced in finding a gracious God. It led to sharp criticism of parts of the Catholic spiritual tradition and new emphases on lay people, the Bible and secular works as opposed to churchly acts of piety. His turbulent personality and earthy language were very different from our stereotypes of the calm, nice, heavenly-minded 'spiritual person'.

Luther's strengths and weaknesses were partly inherited from Augustine. He focused almost exclusively on sin, forgiveness and the cross, with little attention to healing, transformation or resurrection. His low expectation for change in the Christian life has led to large numbers of 'luke-warm' Lutherans. His view that love of self is the opposite of love for God or for neighbour has been very harmful. Yet his accent on grace and freedom are a matchless part of the Christian tradition.

In the century after Luther's death, his followers kept busy defending themselves and his teaching from Roman Catholics and from distortions within the Lutheran Church. This period, sometimes called the 'Orthodox' or 'Confessional' period was a time of systematizing and defending Luther's teaching. Lutheran scholasticism came to base its theology on Aristotle just as Catholic scholastics had done. Sermons came to be highly formal, academic denunciations of the errors of Catholics, Reformed, Enthusiasts and Lutherans who did not follow orthodoxy.

In this setting, a remarkable friendship developed between an older innovator and a young intellectual who became the prince of the Lutheran Orthodox theologians. **Johann Arndt** (1555–1621) was an innovator in the sense that his sermons and writings were not like those of his contemporaries. He was less interested in defending the 'pure doctrine' of Lutheranism than in promoting genuine spiritual renewal in its followers.

His four books of *True Christianity* were a wake-up call to sleepy Lutherans, a prophetic call for awareness of sin, and a challenge to renewal through daily rebirth. He was accused of Catholic and heretical tendencies, and was saved from condemnation only by his young friend **Johann Gerhard** (1582–1637), who had entered the ministry because of Arndt's influence on him at the age of fifteen. Gerhard was not deaf to the call for a

Lutheran piety, as he wrote a small devotional book himself, but the spirit of the age had little time for the affections of the heart, preferring the polemical, the pedantic and the rational.

Arndt laid the foundations for Lutheran Pietism, which would emerge in the late seventeenth century. He appreciated not only Luther's theology but also his experience as a Christian. His contemporaries wanted to codify Luther; Arndt wanted people to discover Luther's experience of Christ. Clinging to Christ alone is the common theme of Luther and Arndt. Just as Luther was appalled by what he found in the parishes, and returned to write the *Small Catechism*, so Arndt deplored the evils of his day and wrote *True Christianity*, which became the most influential book of devotion in the history of Lutheranism.

Luther was a dominating personality for his followers. Even today Lutherans revere and study him more than any other denomination does its founder. He never set out a system, but the vigour of his struggles and the forthrightness of his proclamation have marked not only those who still bear his name, but many others as well.

Yet the Lutheran tradition did not always follow Luther; it did not always even know him. Not until the twentieth century have his works been studied thoroughly. The tradition and the man stand in a dialogue, often in tension.

Reformed Protestantism called for private and public disciplines of Christian life

The Reformed branch of Protestantism began in Switzerland under the leadership of **Ulrich Zwingli** (1484–1531), a contemporary of Luther. Zwingli went even further in his rejection of the Catholic tradition than did Luther, and the two clashed over the meaning and practice of the Lord's Supper at their only meeting, in 1529. Zwingli died shortly thereafter in battle against a Catholic army.

Zwingli wanted only a spirituality of the Word, with little or no emphasis on the liturgy or the sacraments. He put aside Catholic traditions such as the lectionary (Scripture readings appointed for certain days in the church year), vestments, musical instruments and church visual art. All were to him distractions from the central matter: the Word. If the Bible did not command a given practice, that practice was surely an invention of the papists, and ought to be abandoned; it is said that he nailed shut his church organ.

Characteristic of Zwingli's spirituality is an emphasis on both inwardness and scriptural knowledge. He made a sharp distinction between inward and outward discipleship, and regarded only the inward as valuable. Thus the outer was identified with 'the world', and seen as having little value.

What really counted was overcoming human ignorance by teaching the Bible. Thus the aesthetic, sacramental and mystical dimensions of the Catholic tradition were put aside for the sake of a Bible-based rationalism which was to affect many parts of the Reformed tradition, including the Puritans of New England. This part of the Reformed tradition is in tension with a more moderate strand coming from Calvin.

John Calvin (1509–64), a later reformer, barely escaped from France after the authorities learned of his Protestant views. He went out the back door while the authorities knocked on the front! Calvin wanted to be an 'ivory tower' scholar, but the people of Geneva compelled him to settle there and direct the course of their experiment with a new religious and political order. There he inherited the Swiss tradition of Zwingli, who by this time was viewed as a martyr, so Calvin was not able to change it. For example, Calvin wanted weekly Communion services, as his piety was much more eucharistic, but Zwingli's four times a year pattern had already taken hold.

The theology of Calvin is commonly known to include the teaching of predestination (the teaching of God's choice before creation of who should be saved), but the later Calvinism was often quite different from that of Calvin himself in its theological emphasis and its spirituality. Calvin's teaching grew out of a sense of God's sovereignty and love. If humans could not justify themselves, but only God could do so, then it followed logically that the gift of justification was God's to give to the ones who were chosen. The point of predestination for Calvin was the comfort of knowing that one's relationship to God was secure. One did not need to worry about the final judgment; God had already made the choice. Thus the believer could live in confidence, carrying out the will of God without anxiety.

The starting point for Calvin's spirituality was not predestination but the mystical union of the believer with Christ. He taught that humans are joined to Christ in baptism, and that people grow in that union throughout life. Notice that this union is viewed quite differently from that of the mystics in the Catholic or Orthodox traditions. This mystical union is given to all Christians by faith, not as the end of a long road with progressive stages of growth. Thus every Christian is a 'mystic', living in union with Christ, the way Paul speaks of being 'in Christ' in the New Testament.

Calvin spoke of both justification and sanctification as divine gifts in this process. Fully agreeing with Luther that justification was by grace alone, he gave fuller emphasis to the simultaneous gift of sanctification, the theological term for the process by which people become holy.

Calvin places more emphasis on the spiritual disciplines, whereas Luther valued freedom from prescribed practices. Calvin's writing also shows his focus on the community, not just the individual. He doubted the ability of the intellect to know the self and had a high regard for the power of language. Much more, he was awed by the power and sovereignty of God, and God's tenderness: he discussed God both as Father and as Mother of Christians.[4]

The Reformed tradition in Europe, like the Lutheran, went through a period of scholasticism, defining itself doctrinally. The spirituality of Zwingli often overshadowed that of Calvin, and the theology of Calvin was misinterpreted by placing predestination in the spotlight, rather than his ideas about mystical union. The Reformed tradition has kept alive better than some others, however, the concept of public responsibility for Christians. Reformed piety cannot remain indifferent to the sufferings of others in society; Christians have a responsibility for the health of the common life.

Anabaptists called for radical discipleship in small fellowships

The various small groups who differed from both the Catholics and the Lutheran and Reformed churches were of great variety and were persecuted on all sides. Many of them affirmed 'believers' baptism' and were thus called 're-baptizers' or Anabaptists, since most Europeans had already been baptized as infants. Their belief in baptism by immersion sometimes was cruelly parodied, as they were put to death by drowning.

These groups were feared and despised because their teachings not only differed radically from the Catholic–Protestant consensus, but had political, social and economic implications which threatened the government. Some said that direct inspiration from God superseded the teaching of the Bible. They thus seemed to promote spiritual and political anarchy. The radical takeover of the city of Muenster in 1534–35 gave the movement a bad reputation in the eyes of both Catholics and Protestants. Two men took over as 'kings', demanded total conformity to their views, approved of polygamy, and claimed that the kingdom of God had come to earth. Of course many Anabaptists did not approve of this 'kingdom' either.

The common belief among such groups was that infant baptism was invalid; that just as in the New Testament accounts, one needed to choose to be baptized after coming to faith. Then one became a member of a select community, those persecuted by the world, being the only true disciples of Jesus, sharing the practice of the New Testament, including the rejection of public office or fighting in an army. There was great variety among these groups, some being pacifist, others militaristic.

Many of the radical sixteenth-century groups died out, but one which has remained to the present day is that of **Menno Simons** (1496?–1561). He gathered the fragments of various radical groups to form the fellowship we know as the Mennonites. Menno believed that a person in Christ is a new creature, and assumed that those who were converted and baptized would no longer follow the ways of this world, but rather live without serious sin. The community of the church needed to be protected from false teaching and immoral actions by excommunicating those who trespassed. The Amish were the Mennonites who took this church discipline most seriously.

Thus Anabaptist spirituality has developed in the expectation of personal discipleship, separation from the fashions of the world, a strict moral code enforced by a close community, pacifism, simple lifestyle and direct inspiration of the Holy Spirit.

Anglicans were unified by the Book of Common Prayer

The Church of England experienced stormy reversals in the sixteenth century. The extremes of Roman Catholic and Reformed Protestant views produced famous martyrs and even civil war in the following century. It took a long time for the variety of viewpoints to be accommodated, but eventually the Anglican Church embraced wide differences in theological perspective. What has developed out of those experiences in our own day is a view of Anglicanism as a bridge among the Catholic, Protestant and Orthodox traditions. Thus there is some question about classifying this church as Protestant, since it sees itself as catholic in the sense of universal.

The Anglicans want to include as many views as possible within their communion, and have agreed therefore not to be exclusive about theological or ethical views, but to be united in one form of worship: The Book of Common Prayer. Worship has priority over theology as a basis for their unity. As one Anglican puts it, 'The Book of Common Prayer is a rule of life. It is meant to describe, shape, and support the Anglican way of being Christian.'[5]

The emphasis in Anglican spirituality is on the common liturgy, as the context for personal growth. Thomas Cranmer was the first author of the prayer book (1549), but it has gone through many revisions since then. Praying the Psalms is a significant part of Anglican worship, as it followed the liturgy of the monastic hours. The collects or common prayers of this collection reveal Anglican sensibilities and exquisite literary style.

The story of Anglican spirituality beyond the sixteenth century is one which includes many poets. Among the first was **George Herbert** (1593–1633), whose poetry reveals startling images and deep devotion. Herbert is often cited as an Anglican of moderate views. He was a parish priest for a short time and wrote *A Priest to the Temple; or, the Country Parson*, which was published after his death in 1652. This book is an early, profound meditation on pastoral care which has influenced clergy of many denominations in their care of souls.

Another early poet-priest was **John Donne** (1571–1631) who is known for his witty poems based on his convictions concerning the incarnation— he combined flesh and spirit in striking ways. Donne is also remembered for his meditation that 'No man is an island', all of humanity being part of a continent, deeply tied to one another.

Two of the most influential of Anglican divines were **Lancelot Andrewes** (1555–1626) and **Jeremy Taylor** (1613–67). Andrewes has been seen in our generation as an Anglican who embodies the best of Anglican spirituality. He was an influential clergyman in his own day, and later influenced T.S. Eliot, the twentieth-century poet. Taylor's books, *Holy Living* (1650) and *Holy Dying* (1651) are practical guides to devotion, drawing on biblical and patristic sources. Taylor was one of the greatest composers of English prayers.

Early Anglicanism contained the seeds for the three main branches of emphasis which developed more clearly later in its history. The liberal or broad church strand (eighteenth century) emphasized the role of the human intellect in appropriating and expressing the truth of God, found in nature as well as Scripture. The evangelical or low church strand (eighteenth century) emphasized the teachings of the Protestant reformers in Europe, with special emphasis on preaching for conversion and lively singing. The catholic or high church strand (nineteenth century) emphasized the role of bishops and sacraments, the early fathers of the church and continuity with Roman Catholicism.

Anglicans have thus developed a strong tradition of spirituality with many strands. Communal worship stands at the centre; personal piety is practised in that context.

These four types of Protestant churches in the sixteenth century, the Lutherans, the Reformed, the Anabaptists and the Anglicans, were to increase in number and variety as time passed. Today their communions are found around the globe, in various cultural contexts. What all had in common was an emphasis on the Bible and a strong conviction of the need for reform of Roman Catholicism, not only in various abuses, but also in basic principles and common practices of spirituality.

The Catholic Reformation

At the very time that some Catholics were leaving the church in frustration, others were working to curb the abuses which most people agreed were hindering its life. There was a great need for change in the institutional life of the church, and for a response to the theological challenges of the Protestants.

The Council of Trent attempted to deal with both. It met sporadically in northern Italy from 1545 to 1563. The political side of the reforms were difficult. Progress was made, however, in improving education for priests and outlawing abuses by bishops. The office of bishop, for example, could no longer be sold to the highest bidder.

On the theological side, the council drew up doctrinal statements which defined Catholicism as distinct from Protestantism, defending what Protestants had attacked. The conservative, defensive response of Trent is understandable in its context, but is nevertheless regrettable: Catholics and Protestants rejected each other for 400 years thereafter. It was not until Vatican II in the 1960s that the door was opened for serious conversation between these two branches of Christendom.

Ignatius Loyola founded the Jesuits, a new type of religious order

About the same time that Luther was defending his teachings in Germany, **Ignatius Loyola** (1491?–1556) experienced a profound conversion from reading spiritual literature. He was lying recuperating in a hospital after receiving a serious wound in the Battle of Pamplona in 1521 when he read the life of Jesus and lives of the saints. He dedicated himself entirely to Jesus Christ and began writing one of the most powerful books in the history of Christian spirituality, his *Spiritual Exercises*.

After travelling to the Holy Land to fulfil a vow of thanksgiving, Ignatius took up the study of theology in Paris. It was here that a group of like-minded persons gathered around him. This group eventually moved to Rome and received the pope's permission to form a new order, the Society of Jesus, in 1540. Ignatius was elected the superior general, and spent the rest of his life leading the order from its headquarters in Rome.

The *Spiritual Exercises* are really a manual written for a retreat director. The instructions are simultaneously very specific and very flexible. It was intended that the retreatant would spend thirty days, passing through four 'Weeks' during which a number of experiences would lead to discernment of the direction of life for that person. During the retreat the person would meet daily with a spiritual director, pray for four or five hours, participate in the Mass, and keep silence. Ignatius himself, however, encouraged the director to adapt this programme to individual needs, and the retreat is now often given in several shorter periods, except that Jesuits themselves still do the full thirty days.

The paradoxical feature of the *Exercises* is their appeal to the affections or emotions to accomplish their purpose, while remaining very rational. The retreatant's imagination is especially employed to reconstruct biblical scenes, in which the retreatants participate and feel the motions of their hearts. The programme is designed to give individual freedom within a rather clear and fixed pathway, leading to a clear decision about how to follow Jesus. The daily examen (examination of conscience) is an important discipline described in the *Exercises*. It is an exercise in surrender to God and discernment of God's leading.

The Jesuit Order which Ignatius founded was to be a radical new form of monasticism. It went another step beyond the mendicant orders

(Franciscans and Dominicans) to individualize the commitment to a religious order. Whereas 'stability', the promise to stay in one place, was part of monastic vows, the Jesuits saw travel to wherever they were needed as their ascetic duty. Also the ideal of 'contemplative in action' meant that the Jesuit did not always live in community, but was often alone, and for those who were together, there was no chanting of the Divine Office. This departure from the tradition meant that service to others was a higher priority than communal worship. Yet each Jesuit was expected to find time in the day to say his own office, that is, to pray the prayers and read the Scriptures appointed for that day.

Ignatius' ideals were formed partly by St Paul, the same Paul who was the basis for Luther's reformation. But Ignatius and the Jesuits were totally opposed to Lutheranism, and took special vows of loyalty and obedience to the pope. What inspired Ignatius was Paul's lifestyle as a missionary, his willingness to be all things to all people in order to save some.

Ignatius was also influenced by *The Imitation of Christ*, the only book other than the Bible which he recommended in the *Spiritual Exercises*. It is clear, however, that Ignatius had some significant differences from this book, notably in its denigration of academic and intellectual pursuits. His order was to become known for the highest standards of scholarship.

The Jesuits made use of three important practices which they developed to a high degree of usefulness. The retreat, as defined in the *Spiritual Exercises*, was further defined in a *Directory* of 1599. Here the traditional three stages of spiritual life (purgative, illuminative and unitive) were connected with the four weeks of the retreat.

Secondly, spiritual direction became a Jesuit specialty, growing out of the retreats. In later history, Jesuits came to be the confessors or directors for many of the powerful rulers of Europe, and were suspected of using their influence directly for the Pope. Thirdly, a number of sodalities or confraternities were formed in Jesuit schools. These were youth groups which met to encourage spiritual commitment among boys, some of whom would later become Jesuits themselves.

The ideal of travel for service, inspired by the apostle Paul, led many Jesuits to become missionaries to Latin America, Africa, and Asia as well as Europe. Two of the most notable were **Matteo Ricci** (1552–1610) in China and **Roberto de Nobili** (1577–1656) in India. They developed a high regard for their host cultures, and went far (the Pope said too far!) in adapting Christianity to those cultures. As a result they gained adherents from some of the most powerful and well-educated of those societies, but were not able to found lasting churches. This would prove to be a sharp contrast to much later mission history, where the poor and marginal members of society were attracted to Christianity by missionaries who did not much respect the host culture.

The early Jesuit balance between the mystical and the practical proved difficult to maintain after the death of Ignatius. The order veered towards moralism and absolutism, a willingness to deceive and acquire secret information which made it the fear of all Protestant rulers. Persons were accused of being Jesuits, and it was feared that they would try to overthrow Protestant rulers on behalf of Spain or France. Because of political activities the order was suppressed in 1774. It was re-established in 1814 without the political intrigue, and has become the largest single Catholic order in the world.

Teresa of Avila and John of the Cross renewed the Carmelite Order

Mother Teresa of Jesus (1515–82), as her contemporaries called her, is one of the great mystics and reformers of Spain. She had become a Carmelite, an order founded on Mount Carmel in the Holy Land in the mid-twelfth century. Teresa became the leader of a reform movement which followed the early strict rule of the Carmelites, rather than a more recent, mitigated one. The reform movement came to be called 'Discalced' or shoeless. Teresa was involved in founding many new houses of nuns, and in defending the reform to many authorities.

It is as a mystic, however, that she has had her greatest influence. Her *Life* gives a direct view of her trials and development. She describes her severe illness of 1538–39, her conversion to a deep spiritual life in 1554, and the vision of Christ sending a spear through her heart in 1559. The men around her did not know how to deal with her frequent visions and 'locutions' (words from God), and told her they must come from the devil. She was deeply troubled until she obtained sounder advice from another mystic.

The *Interior Castle* is a thoroughgoing analysis of spiritual development. In seven 'mansions', she describes the soul's journey to God, from the purgative, through the illuminative to the unitive. She also classifies prayer, meditation and contemplation. She writes of two kinds of passive contemplation, the prayer of quiet and the prayer of union, which were her daily practice.

Like her younger associate, John of the Cross, she indicates severe trials near the end of this journey. Her prose, however, is much more understandable than John's as she uses metaphors and experiences of daily life to explain her meaning. She also wrote poetry, but John is unequalled in verse.

The writings of **John of the Cross** (1542–91) reflect a life of dramatic reversals. John was invested with considerable responsibility by Teresa even as a young man, when he joined the reform movement in the Carmelite Order. She had already founded the movement among the nuns; he was to found it among the monks. In fact he became for a time the spiritual director of Teresa herself during the time she experienced what she called the 'spiritual marriage'.

He was later kidnapped and imprisoned in a dank cell for six months by his opponents in the order who were against the reform movement. It was in prison that he began to compose poetry, first only mentally, and then on paper. After escaping from prison, he was elected again for responsible posts in the reform branch of the Carmelites, and wrote most of his prose works during the 1580s.

But because of his unwillingness to be a 'whistle-blower', because of stating his frank opinion in a committee meeting with the vicar general of the order, he was stripped of all his offices and sent to an obscure post, where he became ill and died at the age of forty-nine.

Out of this life of passion and conflict, John wrote works on spiritual theology which led to his selection as a doctor of the Roman Catholic Church. His main works are *The Ascent of Mount Carmel*, *The Dark Night of the Soul*, *The Spiritual Canticle*, and *The Living Flame of Love*. These prose works do not enjoy the same esteem as his poetry for stylistic excellence; his explanation of the poetry is often dense and repetitive. Nevertheless his poetry is among the best ever written in the Spanish language. Here is a sample in translation:

> One dark night,
> Fired with love's urgent longings
> —Ah, the sheer grace!—
> I went out unseen,
> My house being now all stilled;

In darkness, and secure,
By the secret ladder, disguised,
—Ah, the sheer grace!
In darkness and concealment,
My house being now all stilled; ...

O guiding night!
O night more lovely than the dawn!
O night that had united
The Lover with His beloved,
Transforming the beloved in her Lover.

Upon my flowering breast
Which I kept wholly for Him alone,
There He lay sleeping,
And I caressing Him
There in a breeze from the fanning cedars.

When the breeze blew from the turret
Parting His hair,
He wounded my neck
With his gentle hand,
Suspending all my senses.

I abandoned and forgot myself,
Laying my face on my Beloved;
All things ceased; I went out from myself,
Leaving my cares
Forgotten among the lilies.[6]

The most distinctive concept for which he is known is the dark night. He uses this metaphor in at least two ways: to describe the inability of the intellect to grasp God; and to describe the experience of the soul on its journey to the mountain top, to union with God.

In the first sense, he is saying something which had become widely accepted in the Middle Ages from the influence of Pseudo-Dionysius: a negative theology which underlined the inadequacy of any concept or image to describe God. In the second, however, he was to give classic expression to the experience of lostness, confusion, drought and panic which is often part of the spiritual path.

Recommended Reading

Ignatius, *Spiritual Exercises*, edited by Robert Bockhouse, Hodder, 1989.

Timothy F. Lull, *Martin Luther's Basic Theological Writings*, Minneapolis: Fortress, 1993.

Frank Senn, editor, *Protestant Spiritual Traditions*, New York: Paulist Press, 1993.

Teresa of Avila, *Complete Works*, edited by E. A. Peers, Sheed and Ward, 1989. (*Classics of Spiritual Writing* Series)

The Collected Works of St John of the Cross, translated by Kieran Kavanaugh and Otilio Rodriguez. Washington, DC: ICS Publications, Institute of Carmelite Studies, 1994.

The 'Modern' Era

In the seventeenth to nineteenth centuries, Christianity faced many new challenges as it began to move from Europe to again become a trans-continental faith. After sputtering attempts by Portuguese and Spanish missionaries in the sixteenth century, Christianity came to the Americas by emigration, and then with a revived zeal, to Africa and Asia by a populist mission movement in the nineteenth century.

Much of Christian attention in this period, however, was focused on European and American problems: new cultural developments, urbanization, the industrial revolution, wars among countries. New approaches to spirituality were developed among the relatively young Protestant churches, and in the Catholic and Orthodox churches as well.

The 'modern' world-view saw itself as 'Enlightenment'

The cultural changes in Europe from the fifteenth to the eighteenth century were so dramatic that people began to see themselves in an entirely new era. They looked back on history now in three main stages—the ancient, the middle (or medieval) and the modern. With the rise of a new style of learning, sometimes called Humanism, in the fifteenth century, the theological method of scholasticism had been put in the shade. The rise of Protestantism ended the sole dominance of the Catholic Church in European culture. The secular interests of the Renaissance separated the spiritual into another sphere.

The full implications of the Renaissance were not realized, however, until the 1700s, when a new movement, identified with rationalist thinkers such as Newton, Voltaire, Kant, Locke and Franklin, emerged. It was later called the Enlightenment. The movement understood itself to be the dawn of a new day after the long night of the Middle Ages. Its implication was that the age of superstition was passing, and human beings now could use the clear-headed guide of their own reason to test every proposition claiming truth.

In the thirteenth century, Aquinas had welcomed reason as the divine gift to accompany and provide the basis for revelation. His synthesis of reason and revelation, nature and grace was one of the great intellectual accomplishments of the Western church. His system was dismantled by the philosophers in such a way that revelation no longer had an independent claim to truth, but had to be submitted to the judgment of what was thought reasonable. For example, miracles were not thought possible, but proving that a rational God existed was thought very reasonable. Yet 'reason' is in fact a variable term; what is thought reasonable at one time varies greatly from another. It was not long before the prevailing proofs of God's existence were challenged.

One contemporary theologian, Darrell Jodock, summarizes the 'modern' with this list of themes: (1) autonomous reason, (2) progress and anti-tradition, (3) objectivity and an infatuation with science, (4) optimism, (5) individualism, and (6) mechanism.[1] The 'modern' world-view saw God as a distant, intelligent designer who set the universe going like a great clock, and then left it to run on its own. Religion was largely reduced to morality, leaving little room for an affective spirituality.

In the late twentieth century many people believe that we are again moving into a new era, and that the modern paradigms of science and philosophy no longer fit our experience. Thus many writers speak of the post-modern era, not yet giving a name to the new age, but indicating that the assumptions which framed the seventeenth to the nineteenth centuries are becoming obsolete. New paradigms demand new theologies and new spiritual styles.

Yet much of our European and North American way of thinking in the twentieth century is still oriented to those assumptions. We are still secularists, separating spirituality from the 'real world', we still tend to think of science as the arbiter of that real world, we are still optimistic about technological progress, and we are still individualists.

It is the period of the Enlightenment, I am convinced, that separates the Western world from the rest of the world. The assumptions and the continuing effects of the Enlightenment make a gap between Christians in Europe and

North America and their brothers and sisters elsewhere. It is important to see how this period has affected Christian spirituality for good or ill.

Protestants regained spiritualities of the heart

After the period of reformation, many of the Protestant movements went through three periods of development. The first was a confessional period, when the attention of the leaders was focused on defining and defending the denomination intellectually. The second was a pietist period, calling for more attention to the needs of ordinary people, especially in the affective dimension of the spiritual life. And finally, the rationalist period or Enlightenment, described above, brought the critique of an autonomous reason to bear on both the Bible and the practices of the churches. Rationalism reduced the role of religion to teaching universal ethical norms, and so had little emphasis on personal relations to God, or the death and resurrection of Jesus.

It should be noted that in the English-speaking world, the periods of pietism and rationalism overlapped; each was competing with, and to some degree influencing the other. For example, John Wesley read John Locke and was very much interested in empirical verification. Across the Atlantic, Benjamin Franklin went to hear the evangelist George Whitefield, and could not prevent himself from contributing all his coins to Whitefield's orphanage project.

Puritans, Quakers and Pietists

The Puritan movement in the Church of England began as early as the 1500s, but continued into the 1700s to Jonathan Edwards, 'the last Puritan'. It was a movement to purify the Anglican church along Reformed Protestant lines. Thus it took its inspiration from the teachings of Zwingli in Zurich and Calvin in Geneva. The popular view of Puritans is thought to be unfair by many of the scholars who have studied the movement. The Puritans were more affirming of human work, play and sexuality than they are given credit for.

The sabbath became the mainspring of the Puritan calendar, as the annual calendar of the Catholic Church with Advent and Lent was discarded. The sabbath was to be devoted to religious pursuits, with emphasis on hearing the Word preached, and on receiving the sacrament of the Lord's Supper.

Puritans did experience raptures that are comparable to those of the Catholic mystics, though they would abhor the comparison. They were also free to use erotic metaphors for these intense experiences, and frequently quoted the Song of Songs or Bernard's spiritualized version in which the lovers are Christ and the soul.

Puritan theology was meant to lead to an assurance that one was indeed predestined (chosen) by God for salvation. Like many other forms of Christian spirituality, the Puritans thought that their life in God was so important that half-way measures were not possible: Christianity demanded the whole of personal and social life.

It was from prison that **John Bunyan** (1628–88) wrote one of the most influential English Christian classics, *Pilgrim's Progress*. As a Puritan he shared the fate of many of his companions. The book is an allegory of the Christian life, using a protagonist named Christian who meets trials and temptations such as Vanity Fair, the Slough of Despond, and the Delectable Mountains on his way to the Celestial City. The basic metaphor of life as a journey is a rich one. It is clear from this story that Bunyan and other Puritans did not see Christian spirituality as a hobby for 'couch potatoes', but as a vigorously challenging struggle with the world and one's own desires. His allegory inflamed the spirituality of Protestants for centuries to come.

Contemporaries of the Puritans and often in conflict with them were the Quakers, the group which called itself the Society of Friends, and which continues its witness for peace up to the present day. There are parallels here to the radical wing of the Reformation in Germany: in both places the new sects were persecuted and feared for undermining religious teaching and threatening the foundations of public order (see Chapter 5).

George Fox (1624–91) the founder of the Quakers, believed that the Holy Spirit spoke directly through people, to what he called 'that of God in every man'. This inspiration seemed to rank higher than the Scripture, and so was opposed by the churches. The charismatic early meetings for worship, without clergy or sacrament, depended on individuals to wait in silence for the inspiration of the Spirit, and to hear what others were led to say.

Quakers in America were distinguished from other Christians by their witness for peace and fair dealing with all peoples. William Penn, founder of

Pennsylvania, is reputed to have dealt more fairly with American Indians than other early colonists did. His Quaker convictions led to a respect for Native people not shown by others.

Later the Quakers were the first Christian denomination to publicly oppose slavery. They were tugged in this direction by the tender conscience of **John Woolman** (1720–72). He came to abhor slavery and spent much of his life personally confronting slave owners and speaking in Quaker meetings. His *Journal* is a book of inspiration still widely read.

The Quakers demonstrate a spirituality which is simple and holistic: social justice actions are not separate from listening to the Spirit. Though we may smile at their refusal to take off their hats or address officials in polite English, the same principles which led to these offensive actions led the Quakers to oppose war and stand for the rights of Indians and African slaves. Their spirituality led them to oppose social convention on all levels, and many early Quakers suffered prison and death for their courageous discipleship.

In Germany Lutheran Pietism was a movement of church reform begun by **Philip Jacob Spener** (1635–1705) under the influence of Arndt. Like Arndt, he saw the church as passive and indifferent, not aware of the true Christianity of the Gospels. Like Arndt he called for self-examination, repentance and conversion. Like Arndt he tired quickly of the polemics which seemed to dominate Lutheran sermons.

What Spener did that went beyond Arndt was to publish a programme of church reform and to organize groups to accomplish it. The book was *Pia Desideria* ('pious hopes'), which unlike its title was very concrete in its proposals. Most of these would not sound radical today. He called for midweek Bible studies, lay activism in the church, sermons that built up the hearer instead of arguing with other preachers or showing off classical learning, seminaries which taught pastoral care. But in his day these were seen as radical, and he faced considerable ostracism, leading even to forced departure from his parish in Frankfurt.

The social side of Pietist reform was developed by **August Herman Francke** (1663–1727), who was not only a professor of theology at Halle, but the founder of institutions for social help. He started orphanages, schools and a library. Francke also trained some of the first Protestant missionaries to leave Europe. Ziegenbalg and Plotschau travelled to India under Danish sponsorship. They made a good start in studying Indian religion and culture, as well as publishing books for India. Later Pietism spread to Scandinavian Europe, led by Hauge, Rosenius and others, and to other continents through missionaries who had been stirred by its call.

Thus the Pietist movement emphasized personal conversion, with the expectation of a renewed life, an outer change coming from inner rebirth. It broke new ground in Bible study for the laity, social institutions and foreign missions. The Pietists insisted that Christianity is a life to be lived and not just a mental faith. The dark side was their tendency to feel self-righteous, and a legalism which made all pleasure something 'worldly'. The remarks of Tertullian on public spectacles would have been approved by strict Pietists.

Evangelicals and Methodists

Similar to the Pietists were the Evangelicals who emerged in the following century in England and New England. The 1700s were an age in which both rationalism (witness the US constitution) and evangelicalism (witness the rise of the Methodists) developed. Evangelicalism seems an obvious foil to rationalism, and yet it shared many of rationalism's assumptions. It had an inquiring practical bent; Wesley was willing, one might say, to do scientific research in the realm of the spiritual by waiting to see which religious experiences were valid and which led nowhere.

We can describe early evangelicals in three settings: the Anglican Church, the Methodist movement, and the Congregationalist churches of New England. What all had in common was preaching for repentance, expectation of a changed life after conversion, and room for expressions of emotion not always tolerated in the previous denominations.

The Anglican branch of this movement was not led by any single person. Perhaps one of the best known is **John Newton** (1725–1807), because he was the author of the beloved hymn 'Amazing grace! how sweet the sound that saved a wretch like me.' Newton had been a captain in the slave trade, was dramatically converted, and became an Anglican priest, dying in the pulpit. Like other Evangelicals, he believed in rising early for prayer, Bible reading as an indispensable part of devotion, and the gathering of the family for group prayers.

In its second generation, Anglican evangelicalism produced one of the outstanding social reformers of the modern era, **William Wilberforce** (1759–1833), whose persistent voice in the British Parliament led to the abolition of the trans-Atlantic slave trade in the early 1800s. His prayer life is said to have given him the perseverance over the decades necessary for the passage of this legislation. A leading member of the 'Clapham Sect', a fellowship of wealthy Evangelicals, he wrote *A Practical View of the Prevailing System of Professed Christians in the Higher and Middle Classes in this Country Contrasted with Real Christianity*.

In the third generation came **Henry Venn** (1796–1873), the general secretary of the Church Mission Society who advocated 'self governing, self-supporting, and self-propagating churches' instead of continued missionary dependency in Africa and Asia. His concept is fundamental to the practice of indigenous Christian spirituality. Ahead of his time, Venn advanced Samuel Ajayi Crowther to be the first African bishop in the Anglican Church. When Crowther died (long after Venn), he was replaced by a European bishop. This led to the founding of some of the first African indigenous churches, whose spirituality was to be much more African.

The Methodist story of the 1700s is full of drama and opposition. **John Wesley** (1703–91) and his brother Charles were uncommonly devoted, partly through the reading of *The Imitation of Christ* and British devotional writers. With a few other students, the Wesleys formed a group for regular prayer, Holy Communion, and prison visitation at Oxford University. The group came to be ridiculed with names such as 'The Holy Club' and 'Methodists'. Their daily timetables and other strict requirements led to this charge of 'Method-ism'. But it was to be years before the Methodists emerged as a Christian denomination.

John and Charles, on their way to be missionaries in Georgia, encountered the Moravians, a group similar to Lutheran Pietists. John made a mess of his work in America, insisting on strict rules and refusing Communion to a woman who left him for another man. He had to leave under threat of arrest. Furthermore, all his righteous striving had not given him peace with God. On his return to England he continued his contact with the Moravians, and at one of their meetings on Aldersgate Street, he was able to come to personal faith in Christ and peace of heart. He described this experience in a famous passage in his *Journal* for 24 May, 1738. Someone was reading from Luther's preface to the epistle to the Romans.

> About a quarter before nine, while he was describing the change which God works in the heart through faith in Christ, I felt my heart strangely warmed. I felt I did trust in Christ, Christ alone for salvation; and an assurance was given me that he had taken away *my* sins, even *mine*, and saved *me* from the law of sin and death.[2]

Ever after this, Wesleyan spirituality has been known as the spirituality of the warm heart. His new emphases gradually made him unwelcome in Anglican Churches. These rejections led John Wesley to begin preaching outside the church buildings in fields and in the streets. His parish, he said, was the world, and he travelled constantly, often preaching five times a day. He said he wanted to spread scriptural holiness over the land. In other words, he looked for practical changes in the lives of the converted.

One of those changes was avoiding gin, which had been the ruin of many families. Instead he encouraged saving money in 'thrift clubs' and wrote pamphlets on improving one's health. These habits took hold among many poor Methodists to such a degree that English society was changed, and the Methodists tended to move out of poverty.

The most contentious teaching of Wesley concerned Christian perfection. Wesley understood the biblical passages on perfection[3] to mean that the work of sanctification could follow justification and lead to perfect love in the intentions of the believer. Furthermore, that some persons experienced this 'entire sanctification' as 'second blessing', an instantaneous experience. Wesley never claimed this for himself, but reported it of several followers.

The spirituality of John Wesley himself was different from that of his followers. He was educated and committed to the Anglican Church. He liked to read the New Testament in Greek and critically read the Eastern Orthodox and Catholic mystics. Frequent Communion was important to him.

But many of the early Methodists were not highly educated, and had little interest in the history of spirituality. Their practical experience was that the Anglican Church, comfortable in its upper class culture, was not especially friendly to them. Reading the Word was more important than attending Communion services. So after his death, the Methodists went against the wishes of John Wesley and formed a separate denomination.

Charles Wesley (1707–88) did not travel as John did. He stayed at home, raised a family, and wrote 5,000 hymns. He was surely one of the greatest of English hymn writers, bringing together biblical language, emotional power and poetic beauty. A spirituality can be expressed in hymns, and Charles' collections surely had much to do with shaping not only Methodist piety but also Protestant devotion throughout the English-speaking world. Evangelical faith whether of Luther or of the Wesleys longs to sing the praise of its Saviour.

> O for a thousand tongues to sing my great Redeemer's praise,
> the glories of my God and King, the triumphs of his grace!

The Wesleyan heritage was to produce many branches, not only the large Methodist churches in the USA, but also the smaller holiness groups founded in the 1800s, such as the Salvation Army and the Church of the Nazarene. The former concentrated on urban evangelism among the poor; the latter on developing the doctrine of complete sanctification (see Chapter 7).

The Oxford Movement called Anglicans to catholic ways

The Church of England received a new impetus towards ancient spiritualities from a movement which began in Oxford about 1830. Some Anglican leaders, deeply disturbed by the incursions of the state into church affairs and by the rationalism which invaded the church at the time of the Enlightenment, proposed a renewal of spiritual life along new lines. Evangelical revival, with its emphasis on individual conversion, did not satisfy the needs they saw in the church.

They emphasized the teachings of the church fathers, the importance of the church as a divine institution, kept by apostolic succession as an organic community of faith. Thus they raised the awareness of the importance of bishops and sacraments and liturgy. They were influenced by the Greek fathers towards views of divinization as the theology of Christian life. All these views were expressed in a series of *Tracts for the Times* (1833—41) from which the group was known as 'Tractarians'. They were very much influenced by the 'Caroline Divines', clergy who served under King Charles in the seventeenth century. Both Herbert and Taylor discussed above are part of this group.

The three most important leaders of the Oxford movement were **John Keble** (1792–1866), **John Henry Newman** (1801–90) and **Edward Pusey** (1800–82). Keble is known as the author of a book of poems, *The Christian Year* (1827). He had considerable influence on Newman as a professor of poetry at Oxford. Newman, an evangelical in early days, became a high church proponent, and then broke with the Anglican Church in 1845 to become a Roman Catholic. He was made priest and cardinal of the Catholic Church in England. A great scholar, he nevertheless was very pragmatic about the disciplines of prayer. Pusey was also a scholar, a Professor of Hebrew. Followers of the movement were sometimes called 'Puseyites'. Like the others, he often quoted the Greek and Latin fathers, but also know the Syriac writers, such as Ephrem. He knew the spiritual writers discussed in this book very well, and edited a series of translations of the fathers. He revived the practice of sacramental confession in the Anglican Church, and was much sought after as a spiritual director. He also helped to found Anglican religious orders, parallel to the Roman Catholic ones, such as the Benedictines.

French Roman Catholics enhanced spiritual direction

There were a number of French Catholic spiritual writers in the modern period whose influence has gone beyond France and beyond the Catholic Church. The first of these was **St Francis de Sales** (1567–1622), whose *Introduction to the Devout Life* is still in print.

As Catholic bishop of Geneva, Switzerland, de Sales was very much involved both in preaching Catholic Reformation tenets from the Council of Trent and in giving spiritual direction to individuals. He came to write the *Introduction* as a means of reaching many others, and his clear style and use of many illustrations showed his intent that 'devotion' or holiness was for everyone, not just the clergy or religious. He corresponded with Jane de Chantal and others who became spiritual directors in their own right.

His teaching is positive in tone, one might say optimistic, but his underlying intent is very serious. De Sales made a clear distinction between the will and the emotions. For him the commitment of the will to God was to be resolute, whatever the emotional distractions.

Cardinal Pierre de Berulle (1575–1629), called the founder of the 'French School' of spirituality, was influenced by personal contact with de Sales and by reading the church fathers, Ruysbroeck and St Teresa of Avila. He helped to introduce St Teresa's Discalced Carmelites into France. The most important feature of his spirituality is Christocentrism, that is, its focus on Jesus Christ. The incarnation and the eucharistic presence of Christ are central. Unlike de Sales, however, Berulle and the French School tend to be pessimistic about human nature and severe in ascetic practice.

Nicholas Hermon, better known as **Lawrence of the Resurrection** (1611–91), was a lay brother in the Discalced Carmelites. His work in the kitchen did not draw much attention until the time of his death, when his superior interviewed him concerning his spirituality. Those interviews together with letters found after his death constitute the little devotional classic, *The Practice of the Presence of God*. Brother Lawrence describes how he focused on God not simply at quiet hours of prayer, but in the midst of his daily work: washing pots and pans.

> My most ordinary state is this simple attention, and this general, loving gaze upon God, to which I often find myself attached by sweetness and satisfaction greater than that which a baby feels at the breast of his nurse. If I dared to use the expression, I would willingly call this state 'the breast of God', because of the inexpressible sweetness that I taste and experience in it.[4]

One of the greatest influences of the French school on popular piety was devotion to the Sacred Hearts of Jesus and Mary, developed by **St John Eudes** (1601–80). These were devotional movements emphasizing the humanity of these exalted figures. The theme of the heart was a reference to the love of Jesus and of Mary towards the faithful, by the passion of the cross.

Later developments in France led to the denunciation of both Quietism and Jansenism by the Catholic Church. The complexities of these movements make them impossible to describe within the limits of our space. The roots of Quietism go back at least to **Miguel de Molinos** (b. 1628), who, for reasons that are not clear, was condemned by Pope Innocent XI. Molinos seems to have taught such an abandonment to God that all things become indifferent to the soul, including the soul's own salvation, and thus, ultimately the soul's relation to God. Thus the love of God paradoxically produces indifference to God. This is the view condemned as Quietism.

Accused of a similar teaching were **Mme Jeanne-Marie Bouvier de la Mothe Guyon** (1648–1717) and her advisor **François Fenelon** (1651–1715), Archbishop of Cambrai, in France. Fenelon came to be accepted into the highest circles of French Society, in charge of the education of King Louis XIV's grandsons. He introduced Mme Guyon to these circles, but when her writing were condemned, he refused to join in attacks on her character, and for this was exiled from the court completely. She spent four years in the Bastille and he was forced into obscurity.[5] He wrote a courageous letter to Louis XIV, frankly denouncing his war policies which brought suffering to so many for the sake of the king's personal glory.

Fenelon was involved in spiritual direction by letter, like his admired predecessor, Francis de Sales. Because this advice was not lost in oral speech, but preserved in writing, his advice still speaks to twentieth-century Christians. He is especially helpful for those of us who are continually too hard on ourselves:

'Just as water quenches fire so do scruples act on prayer': whenever I think of you, Madame, those words come into my mind... Every time you insist, against your better judgment, on undertaking these self-examinations which have been so often condemned you disturb and upset yourself, dry yourself up, make prayer impossible and so remove yourself from God... You are also taken up almost exclusively with yourself. Tell me, can all this be the work of God?... You should employ that delicate scrupulosity of yours against your own scruples and ask yourself if it can be right under protest of discovering minute faults of behaviour to cause the well-springs of grace emanating from prayer to dry up, and to commit crass errors in order to subtilize little ones.[6]

Fenelon had a great deal to say about abandonment to God, which he describes this way: 'True abandonment simply means letting oneself fall into the arms of God as a child falls into the arms of its mother.'[7]

Jeanne Guyon was theologically uneducated but very sensitive spiritually. She has been decried as 'hysterical' by many writers then and since, but there may be implicit sexism in these judgments. Her willingness to express all of her feelings in her writings, sometimes in excessive ways, weakened her defence; she and Fenelon were declared guilty of Quietism.

Those condemned as Quietists focused on the abandonment to God's providence, the passive reception of God's grace. The Jansenists, on the other hand, who were involved in the condemnation of the Quietists, rather concentrated on the active working out of one's salvation. The moral purpose in Christian living was emphasized, in spite of a renewed teaching of Augustine's doctrine of predestination. It was predestination which ultimately led to the condemnation of the Jansenists also. The Jesuits, strong defenders of free will since Reformation times, were vigorous opponents of Jansenism. It was from a Jansenist background that a distinctive French writer emerged, Blaise Pascal.

Pascal and Kierkegaard developed a new view of selfhood

Two writers who seem to stand apart from their traditions and do not easily fit any of the groups we have spoken about are Blaise Pascal and Søren

Kierkegaard. **Blaise Pascal** (1623–62), who lived in France, was a brilliant scientist and mathematician. Both writers have been seen as influential founders of the existentialist movement in the twentieth century, but neither shares the views of twentieth-century existentialists.

Like Kierkegaard, Pascal exercised outstanding literary ability; his *Provincial Letters* are still studied as models of French style. He gathered fragments of ideas for a rational defence of the Christian faith which was published after his death as *Pensées* (thoughts). In these writings his stance was that of the individual awed by the wonders of the universe, trying to decide whether to trust the Christian message or not. He wrote of the wager that every human being must make, betting one's life on the truth of the faith. He argued that it was better to live as a Christian and be disappointed after death than to live as an atheist and be wrong in the end.

Pascal is well known for his line, 'The heart has its reasons of which reason knows nothing'.[8] By saying this he was rejecting the narrowing of evidence for the creator and redeemer. Pascal was a layperson not trained in theology, and he did not have wide influence in his own day, but his remarks have been treasured not only in France but throughout the Christian world.

A lonely Danish Protestant voice of the nineteenth century takes a similar but distinctive stance on Christian spirituality. **Søren Kierkegaard** (1813–55) was a loner from his youth. After studying theology and philosophy he came to reject both the reigning philosophy, that of Hegel, and the dominant form of Christianity, the Lutheran folk church. He could not identify with the intellectuals or with the Pietists. Rather, after breaking his engagement with Regina Olson, he wrote some forty books in fifteen years which he later called his 'authorship'. On the one hand, the books attacked the reigning orthodoxies and set out his own new philosophy, and on the other, developed 'edifying discourses' for the individual believer.

The former set of books was written pseudonymously, under a variety of names, with marvellous literary and philosophical skill. In those books he sets forth not only a new way of thinking about historical and philosophical problems, but also his doctrine of the three stages of life. He does not write about the stages, but from within them. That is, he assumes the standpoint of each stage in the writer, and demonstrates what the world looks like from that point of view.

He exemplifies the aesthetic stage in Volume 1 of *Either/Or*, a collection of writings including 'The Diary of a Seducer'. This stage views life in terms of pain and pleasure only. Then in Volume 2 he demonstrates the moral stage through the writings of a judge about his marriage. Here the categories become right and wrong. And finally he writes of a religious stage, which takes the holy as the primary category, but includes the aesthetic and moral within it. The religious stage which Kierkegaard points to as necessary is that of the 'knight of faith', the individual who breaks out from the stifling crowd to follow God whatever the cost.

This is a radically different proposal from the traditional three stages of the mystical life. It is a change in consciousness demonstrated by characters. There is no explicit discussion of union with God, but rather trusting God without evidence, which Kierkegaard compares to floating over 50,000 fathoms of water.

The second type of book in Kierkegaard's 'authorship' is devoted to edifying discourses. These books call on Kierkegaard's beloved reader, the individual, to ponder short passages of Scripture. Significant metaphors appear in these writings, such as the rich prince who loves the poor woman and wants to court her, but cannot do so from his magnificent carriage. He must become poor to woo her. This becomes a model of the incarnation. One of Kierkegaard's famous titles which has become an epigram in our day is *Purity of Heart is to Will One Thing*. Kierkegaard calls upon his reader to become a real self. He sees selfhood not as a given, not to be taken for granted. Rather 'I' must become a self through the choices I make.

He was a harsh critic of the Lutheran Church of his day, and was not liked. Although he was Lutheran in his understanding of justification, he scathingly charged that Lutheran free grace was being misappropriated, taken for granted, in a system where everyone assumed themselves to be Christian. Thus one's Christianity became an easy, unimportant matter. On the contrary, Kierkegaard amazed everyone by saying he was *not* a Christian, that this title was too high for him to claim. He hoped to make people stop and think about the commitment entailed in being a Christian.

He was an intellectual, and many of his philosophical works are difficult to understand. But his edifying discourses are written simply and directly. They are difficult, not because of terminology, but because of their demands on the will and the affections.

What is missing in Kierkegaard is a sense of the communal character of Christian faith. Because of his own life experience, he drew a picture of Christian spirituality which was individualist in the extreme. Further, the issues which engaged him did not include the relationship to non-human creation. Thus he is mostly focused on relationships to God and self.

One of the many valuable features of Kierkegaard, however, is his ability to skewer façades of spirituality. It is a special danger for people who *study* spirituality to think they are *living* it. His disdain for preachers dressed in fine robes, preaching about the crucifixion to make money, also applies to the aesthete who dabbles in spirituality as a sort of interesting hobby.

Orthodoxy produced the Philokalia *and* The Way of a Pilgrim

Eastern Orthodox spirituality has a way of drawing upon its holy tradition which renews it age after age. Under the rule of Muslim Turks, long after the death of the Byzantine Empire, the Greek church renewed itself by reading the collection assembled by **Nicodemus of the Holy Mountain** (1749–1809) and **Macarius of Corinth** (1731–1805). This collection, entitled *Philokalia*, ('the love of beauty') drew upon writers in Eastern Christendom from the fourth to the fifteenth centuries. Among its themes were the Jesus Prayer, the need for personal spiritual direction, and the virtues needed not only by monks but by lay people who seek to know union with God. The book, first published in 1782, was soon translated into Slavonic and Russian, but only recently into English. It has become perhaps the most influential book in Orthodox spirituality up to the present day. Its teachings follow Evagrius, but surprisingly do not include any writings by the Cappadocians or Pseudo-Dionysius.

This multi-volume set was expensive and not readily accessible. Most people in Russia were not able to afford it. But one anonymous writer popularized its message in a much shorter work: *The Way of a Pilgrim*. It appeared in 1884, and has remained the popular approach to the Jesus Prayer ever since.

The book tells of the longing of a Russian pilgrim to know the meaning of the constant prayer which Paul counsels in 1 Thessalonians 5:17, 'Pray constantly'. Since the book is a narrative, the reader's interest is focused on what will happen next, as the pilgrim seeks help for over a year and finally finds what he seeks with an old man who says,

> But what is prayer? And how does one learn to pray? Upon these questions, primary and essential as they are, one very rarely gets any

precise enlightenment from present-day preachers... The continuous interior prayer of Jesus is a constant uninterrupted calling upon the divine Name of Jesus with the lips, in the spirit, in the heart; while forming a mental picture of His constant presence, and imploring His grace, during every occupation, at all times, in all places, even during sleep. The appeal is couched in these terms, 'Lord Jesus Christ, have mercy on me.' One who accustoms himself to this appeal experiences as a result so deep a consolation and so great a need to offer the prayer always, that he can no longer live without it, and it will continue to voice itself within him of its own accord. Now do you understand what prayer without ceasing is?[9]

His adventures while praying constantly are more interesting than other writers' long theological discussions of the meaning of the prayer. The book has now been translated into many languages, and is available in English.

Mission spirituality motivated cross-cultural ministry

The earlier Catholic missions of the sixteenth and seventeenth centuries had not planted lasting churches for a number of reasons. In spite of a few notable exceptions among the Jesuits, the mission stations were often staffed by unworthy personnel, who had no training or preparation for the work, and little or no support from their orders. Further, the mission work was an ancillary arm of nationalist imperialism, so that control by Spain or Portugal, or gaining wealth by gold or slaves, was higher in priority than proclaiming the Saviour. Thus most of the sixteenth-century churches in Africa and the Americas died out.

There were a few outstanding missionaries who spoke out against the abuses of soldiers and traders, such as Bartholomew de las Casas, whose writings remain today as the most severe indictment of the Spanish treatment of American Indians. Others such as Jean de Breboef suffered on the nomadic trails of the Great Lakes, patiently learning the Huron language, only to be captured by the Hurons' enemies and tortured to death.

The unshakable conviction of those early Catholic missionaries, and the continuing basis for the missions from Europe and North America that came later was the conviction that salvation was only possible for the world's people if they heard the word of the cross, believed its message, were baptized and became part of the church. This led most of them to overlook the damage which was done to native cultures by Europeans.

Both missionaries and the peoples among whom they served assumed that religion and culture were fixed together in such a way that becoming European was essential to becoming Christian. This is an assumption like that of early Jewish Christians who demanded that Gentile converts become Jews before they could be Christian. Paul passionately disagreed. So do I. This book asserts that it is possible to be authentically Christian in any culture. There will indeed be tension between Christianity and any culture (if the Christian message is not watered down and domesticated too much by economic or political interests), but there will also be gifts that every culture can bring to the understanding of Christianity, just as Christianity has the gift of the good news of God's love for every culture.

Eastern Orthodox missionaries had earlier spread the faith from the Mediterranean into the Slavic lands. Their new outreach was to the east in Siberia, and by the 1700s to Alaska.

Protestants did not get involved in overseas missions until more than a century after the Reformation. Finally with the emergence of Pietism the continental Moravians and Lutherans began sending missionaries in the 1700s. In Great Britain it was **William Carey** (1761–1834) who began the effort. As a young Baptist shoemaker he came to the conviction that God wanted him to travel to India with the message of Christ. His elders assured him that it could not be done, and that if God wanted it done, he surely would not choose *you*, young man! But Carey pressed on, actually travelling to India himself.

Why did the missionaries go, often at great discomfort and danger to themselves? Of course there were unworthy reasons, as all human decisions are ambiguous. But on the positive side, missionary spirituality included love for the people served, courage in facing the unknown, confidence in God's provision when human help often failed, and ultimately, a sense of humour over the tangled human condition, with all its different customs and languages.

For Catholics it was mainly members of religious orders who travelled. Until the late nineteenth century the vast majority were men. They belonged to some of the orders we have already spoken about—the Jesuits, the Franciscans, the Dominicans. But new orders were founded in the nineteenth century, specifically for mission work. The Society for Mission to Africa, or 'White Fathers' is an example.

On the Protestant side, mission societies took up the work before denominations did. The Church Mission Society of the Anglicans was one of the first in 1799. The first American society was founded in 1814. American women became especially active in the late 1800s, founding their own societies and sending single women as well as married ones to serve all over the world. Women gave sacrificially for the support of their missionaries. The women missionaries themselves were often able to fulfil responsible posts which were denied to them at home. Eventually these societies were induced to unite with general societies and the special role of women was gradually lost.

Missionary spirituality includes the spirituality of the missionaries themselves, but also that of their supporters at home. A certain global perspective is one aspect of such a spirituality. Another is fervent prayer, especially intercessory prayer.

The analogue to missionary spirituality is that of the peoples who were first won to Christianity through their efforts. Unfortunately very little of their spirituality has come down to us. It is in the twentieth century that most of the indigenous Christian movements in different continents have developed a distinctive voice. To that century we turn next.

Recommended Reading

David J. Bosch, *Transforming Mission: Paradigm Shifts in Theology of Mission*, Maryknoll, New York: Orbis, 1995.

Peter C. Erb, editor, *Pietists: Selected Writings*, SCM Press, 1993. (*Classics of Western Spirituality* Series)

Francis de Sales, *Introduction to the Devout Life*, A. Clarke Books, 1990.

Anne Fremantle, editor, *The Protestant Mystics*, New York: New American Library, 1964.

Life of Madame Guyon, Cambridge: J. Clarke, 1961.

Philip Jacob Spener, *Pia Desideria*, Minneapolis: Fortress, 1989 (1964).

Douglas V. Steere, editor, *Quaker Spirituality: Selected Writings*, New York: SCM Press, 1984. (*Classics of Western Spirituality* Series)

The Way of a Pilgrim and The Pilgrim Continues His Way, translated by R.M. French, New York: Seabury, 1952.

The Twentieth Century

As we approach the end of the twentieth century, its beginnings seem far in the past. So much has changed in so few decades. In Europe and America we have gone from optimism to despair and back several times. We have been disillusioned by two world wars and a great depression. We have seen the horrors of Auschwitz and Hiroshima, we have heard of Stalin's genocide in the Ukraine. We have lived under the mushroom cloud, and seen the Soviet Empire rise and fall. We have travelled to the moon, and seen the beauty of the earth from space. It is a beauty we perceive to be threatened by ecological disaster. The population of the earth has increased sixfold, along with hunger, malnutrition and poverty. Christianity has spread to about one third of the human population, making its biggest gains this century in Africa.

A new consciousness has been emerging in this century. We are looking at reason and science with more nuanced valuation. We are struggling to find new gender balance in our understanding, new psychological appreciation for the depths of the human, introduced to us by Freud, Jung and others.

The churches of the world have developed new ecumenical relationships since a famous meeting of missionaries in 1910 in Edinburgh. Now the World Council of Churches is a half-century old. The Catholic Church has changed since the Second Vatican Council in the 1960s from monolithic isolation to dialogue with other Christians, with modern society and with other religions.

We live in a world much more closely connected by communications media and by economic interdependence than the world at the start of the century. But we have not made very much progress towards eliminating war or poverty. The Arab-Israeli dispute continues. South Africa has achieved a non-racial democracy, but progress is continually hindered by the shadows of the past. African populations throughout the continent are stirring for more democracy after almost a half-century of independent, but authoritarian governments.

The challenges Christians face at this time are immensely complex, but many of them are the same fundamental problems faced throughout the history of the faith. How are we to 'mend' a creation which is ripped and torn? How are we to live faithfully before a holy God, who redeems and sanctifies us? How shall we face the continuing threats of the powers of evil and the heavy weight of personal and communal guilt? How are we to build community, proclaim the gospel, and protect those at the margins of society from injustice, disease and illiteracy? What does it mean concretely for us to live to the glory of God?

There are a number of movements and individuals who have addressed these and newer issues in our century. I will describe a small sample. The number of people to choose from seems to grow geometrically as we come closer to our own time. In this chapter I will include first two major movements which have affected all continents, Pentecostalism and ecumenism, then a few samples from each continent.

The charismatic dimension re-emerged in Pentecostalism and Neo-Pentecostalism

Pentecostalism was consciously founded as a re-enactment of primitive Christianity as seen in the Acts of the Apostles. The experience of the earliest church seemed such a contrast to what was observed in twentieth-century churches. This was not the first or the last attempt to recapture the harmony and power of primitive Christianity. For example, the restorationist movement of the past century in the USA had led the Disciples of Christ and Churches of Christ to attempt to free the church of denominationalism and to worship as the earliest Christians worshipped. The Society of Brothers, a community founded in Germany in 1920, saw the key to early Christian authenticity in the sharing of goods, pacifism and group discipline.

The immediate antecedents of the Pentecostals were the Holiness Movements, para-church organizations such as the Keswick Convention in Britain which continued Wesley's teaching of entire sanctification when the Methodist churches had lost interest in it. Many felt a longing for 'something more' than the justification by grace they had experienced at conversion. They lacked the power to live the new life expected by these groups, a life of holiness, avoiding the pleasures of the world and devoting themselves to evangelism and social reform.

What was new in Pentecostalism was the identification of Wesley's 'second blessing' with the biblical 'baptism in/with the Holy Spirit'.[1] Furthermore the outward sign of the baptism was speaking in tongues followed by the 'spiritual gifts' listed by Paul in 1 Corinthians 12, among them prophecy and healing.

The pivotal moment in the development of a new style of Christian spirituality was in a store-front church on Azusa Street in Los Angeles in 1906. At that time a black evangelist, **William Seymour** (1870–1922), introduced both black and white seekers to 'baptism with the Holy Spirit' and speaking in tongues. The movement spread with lightning speed, and grew quickly in North and South America. Today it is claimed that Pentecostal denominations are the fastest growing part of Christianity.

Earliest Pentecostalism was multi-racial, but as the movement spread and solidified into denominations, black and white generally organized separately. They were despised and rejected by the established churches because they were mostly poor, uneducated people. Pentacostalists charged that the churches had lost the power of the Holy Spirit. Over the decades Pentecostalism became more moderate as its members gained in affluence, just as Wesley's followers had. They began to found colleges and build handsome churches. The more extreme emotional outbursts in services, which had led to their nickname, 'Holy Rollers', were not so frequent.

Finally, they came to recognize genuine spiritual gifts in members of the so-called mainline denominations. In the 1960s and 1970s large numbers of Protestants and Catholics, and even a few Orthodox Christians were led by the Neo-Pentecostal or Charismatic Movement to the same experiences as 'classical' Pentecostalism. Unlike the people affected in the first few decades of this century, these Charismatics remained in their historic denominations instead of starting new ones. They did not necessarily accept the fundamentalism and the list of forbidden activities of the original Pentecostals. But they did begin to take evangelism, healing and praise very seriously. The movement had its greatest success, surprisingly, among Roman Catholics. The hierarchy saw to it that priestly guidance was given to an essentially lay movement, which began in universities. Cardinal Suenens and Pope Paul VI blessed the movement.

The Protestant churches reacted much more cautiously and sometimes with hostility. The more conservative churches were, surprisingly, the most critical. The Lutheran Church—Missouri Synod—for example, defrocked some of its clergy for their participation. Para-church organizations demanded signed statements from employees that they would not speak in tongues.

What is Pentecostal or Charismatic spirituality? It focuses on the love of God seen to be present and active. The practice of speaking in tongues is experienced as an assurance of God's love. 'Letting go' to allow the Spirit to guide the sounds from the mouth is a form of surrender to God. Answers to prayers for healing of physical or emotional problems likewise underline the presence and power of God. The Holy Spirit, brought into prominence in this movement, nevertheless takes second place to Christ as the Saviour and Friend of the worshipper. The group is the locus for hearing the Word of God both through Scripture and 'prophecy'. Prophecies are often cast in the form of the biblical prophets, 'My people, hear my voice...'. It is understood that God is actively communicating with the group, in these spontaneous messages, which are subject to the norms of Scripture and the judgment of the leadership. In this way the movement is similar to the Quaker form of worship.

The traditional suspicion of education and intellectual endeavour in the earliest Pentacostalists has diminished, especially among Neo-Pentecostalists, but there is still a sense that the anointing of the Spirit is more important than academic degrees for leadership.

A few Charismatic persons took dramatic steps to help the poor as the result of their spiritual renewal. But as a whole the movement did not make care for the poor or advocacy for the oppressed a major theme. The prophecies rarely had the authentic challenge for justice found in the Hebrew prophets, but instead focused on inner assurance of God's love or challenges to religious duties within the group. Thus the movement came in some instances to meet the real need of American Christians for an emotional and experiential faith, but it did not challenge their social or political involvement. The movement definitely led to ecumenical exchanges between surprising partners, notably the Pentecostals and Roman Catholics. But it also in some places was divisive of congregations.

Today there are thousands of Catholics and Protestants who have experienced 'baptism in the Spirit' and speaking in tongues who are no longer active in the Charismatic movement. These people are sometimes continuing a renewed involvement in the churches and even using the gift of tongues in private devotion. They have become a hidden part of the denominations that is interested and inquiring for more instruction in spirituality than the church has given.

Ecumenical spirituality drew churches together

The movement for Christian unity known as ecumenism did not begin in the twentieth century. Ever since there have been divisions in the churches there have been those who have prayed for their reunion. Philip Melanchthon, the young associate of Luther, tried hard to reconcile Lutherans with others. But in the present century ecumenism has developed not only major institutions but widespread themes for prayer among denominations. The institutions of ecumenism include the Evangelical Alliance, the World Missionary Federation, the Faith and Order movement, the Life and Work conferences, the World Council of Churches (1948), etc.

What is of special interest to us here is the growth of a movement of prayer for Christian unity. A week specially devoted to this cause was started in 1908, then approved by Pope Pius X in 1909. At that time many Protestants understood Roman Catholic ecumenism to mean that Protestants should 'come home' to Rome. But **Abbé Paul Couterier** (1881–1953), who was experienced in building understanding between French Catholics and Reformed churches, was able to convince Protestants to adopt the same week, 18–25 January, for the purpose of prayer for unity. Since 1966 the Vatican and the World Council have planned and promoted the week together.

Orthodox, Catholics and Protestants in the present century have learned to pray together on many levels at meetings, conferences and retreats. Many believe that it is only prayer that has kept the movement going in spite of many obstacles. As yet there has been little approved sharing of Holy Communion, but a great deal of inter-communion has taken place informally.

A very special expression of ecumenical spirituality is the community of Taize in France. Founded by Roger Schutz and Max Thurien, it is a semi-monastic order with members from both Catholic and Protestant traditions. The Orthodox have also made their contribution. At a service led by Brother Roger in a packed Episcopal cathedral in Edinburgh, I watched as many non-Orthodox believers joined in kissing a large cross-shaped icon lying in the middle of the church floor, as a prayer of solidarity with Russian Christians.

It could be argued that the Protestant ecumenical movement was begun by missionaries, taken over in mid-century by liberal bureaucrats, and forced to stretch in the second half of the century by Third World Christians and Orthodox and Catholic partners. The presence of the Orthodox churches in the World Council was followed by Vatican II declarations on Ecumenism. After the 1960s ecumenism was changed from an inter-Protestant, largely European and North American affair into something truly ecumenical, that is world-wide.

Conservative evangelicals, long distrustful of the WCC, may never become members, but there is an increasing recognition on both sides of the need to talk instead of ignoring or vilifying each other.

As we turn now to many of the continents of the world, I want to emphasize my belief that the Western world, the so-called first world, needs the two-thirds world, or so-called third world, in order to develop an authentic and vital spirituality. A very good general guide to this process is William Dyrness' book, *Learning about Theology from the Third World*.[2] His focus is on theology, but theology does overlap with Christian spirituality, and the general picture he gives is a helpful expansion of our horizons. Dyrness describes African theology as focused on Christianity and culture, Latin American theology centring on the political setting, and Asian theology discerning the transcendent as its main theme. These are over-generalizations as the author realizes.

His point, however, is that Christians in the West can no longer afford to ignore the contributions and challenges of Christians from these continents. That is, these Christians have both gifts to offer from their own cultural backgrounds and hard questions to ask of the affluent Christians of the West.

More directly related to spirituality is *Common Journey, Different Paths: Spiritual Direction in Cross-Cultural Perspective*.[3] This collection of articles by spiritual directors on different continents explores the issues of multi-cultural communication by sharing the experiences of Catholic spiritual directors.

Whereas the numbers of Christians in Europe and North America show little increase, in these continents Christianity is growing rapidly, and mission societies are being founded to evangelize other countries, including the West. The very vitality of these Christians is a refreshment to the tired churches in secularized, affluent countries. *Christianity Rediscovered*[4] tells of the power of a simple gospel among the Masai in East Africa. Such rediscoveries are also needed in countries where Christianity has long been present.

Latin America

Roman Catholic Christianity came to Latin America with the conquistadors and since then has spread at least nominally to the vast majority of the population. In many countries the ordinary people did not understand the faith and it became an overlay on their previous beliefs. Furthermore, the church came to be a bastion of support for the European populations which held and still hold the land and economic power. In some countries 2 per cent of the people own 90 per cent of the land. The question of social justice was muffled by the cultural captivity of the hierarchy.

But in the mid-twentieth century 'base Christian communities' were started which involved the poor people in Bible-based group meetings which enlivened faith and called into question the economic order. The *campesinos* or peasants learned to read and to think critically about their lives. This grass roots movement is what gave birth to a new kind of theology, liberation theology.

Liberation theology eventually was adopted by professional theologians, and is now well-known throughout the world. It advocates a new way of doing theology, from the perspective of the poor, from the 'bottom up'. It employs Marxist analysis to reveal the injustice and conflict in the human situation, then the Christian gospel to promise hope for liberation from oppression in the historical future. This theology has been criticized from both Catholic and Protestant conservative perspectives on a number of accounts. It has seemed to some to tend towards a secular theology of social and economic revolution without any transcendent or specifically spiritual content.

Gustavo Gutierrez (b. 1928) in *We Drink from Our Own Wells* describes a liberation spirituality which must give the critics pause. His book is valuable in many ways. On the basis of the Latin American poor, he finds traditional Catholic spirituality to fall short on two counts: it is geared to a minority, namely the religious orders, and it is too individualist and interior. What is needed is a spirituality for all the people which includes practical action for liberation on a communal level. Drawing on the Bible and on selected figures from the history of European spirituality, Gutierrez calls for a holistic view of the Christian life, consisting of a trinitarian 'Encounter with the Lord, Walking in the Spirit, and a Journey to the Father'.

For Protestants one of the attractive features of the book is the seriousness with which Gutierrez takes the Bible. In the course of his discussion he also deals at length with Paul's understanding of flesh, spirit and body. He shows that Paul is not following Neo-Platonist denigration of the body, but is using the term flesh in a different sense. This section would be helpful in many books on spirituality, and it is unfortunate that these findings of critical word study were not available centuries earlier.

The special marks of liberation spirituality as set forth in this book are conversion (the necessary break with the past which occurs again and again), gratuitousness (the free, unearned grace of God), joy in suffering and martyrdom (which come in the struggle for liberation), spiritual childhood (which he sees as necessary for a commitment to the poor), and community (as the proper context for solitude).

The problematic elements of liberation theology hardly appear in Gutierrez's book. There is nothing of Marxist analysis here. It is clear that spirituality is for personal and communal relationship to God, and not simply for political revolution. Gutierrez is known as a theologian who lives simply among the people, practising what he advocates in his writing. Similar in tone is Jon Sobrino's *Spirituality of Liberation*.[5] This book is a fresh and serious challenge to others in their own settings to rethink spirituality on biblical, liberationist lines.

The challenge of liberation spirituality for wealthy Westerners is twofold. Is our spirituality so individualized and psychologized that it excludes issues of justice? Are we prepared to share power with groups which have been disempowered, either within our own societies or in the two-thirds world?

Africa

There are two main developments in African spirituality which I would raise for your consideration: the first, liberation concepts in the African setting; and the second, the movement to contextualize African Christianity.

The first movement finds a very similar expression to that of Gutierrez in the volume by Archbishop **Bukole Wa Ilunga** (b. 1920), *Paths of Liberation: A Third World Spirituality*. Both are Catholic authors who in the post-Vatican II setting give considerable attention to the Bible. Both are proposing serious changes for their countries on the basis of experience of oppression and the longing for freedom. Ilunga expresses the essence of freedom as that which enhances life, a central theme in many accounts of African traditions.

The first third of Ilunga's book is a frank discussion of the problems of Zaire. He not only decries the damage to his people brought by years of colonial alienation and present foreign manipulation, but lays out the responsibility of present-day Zairians for the crushing poverty of the country. President Mobutu's policy of 'authenticity' is criticized for not leading back to true African roots, but becoming a political shibboleth behind which all sorts of schemes to defraud people can succeed. The growth of government corruption leading to paralysis of the economy is frankly described, both on high and low levels. The root problem, Ilunga concludes, is human sin: 'the underlying cause of all the things that do not work'.[6]

His prescription, based on a lengthy discussion of the Bible, is that personal liberation must go hand in hand with social, political liberation. If individuals are not freed from sin, even the most just system will not liberate the poor.

Under the banner of black theology, significant development of the liberation theme has taken place in southern Africa. The black theology and black consciousness movements in tandem with similar movements in the USA have articulated a theological opposition to the apartheid system. This system has roots far back in the immigration of Europeans to South Africa since 1652. It was codified into law following the victory of the Nationalist Party in 1948. Apartheid is an Afrikaans word which means 'separateness'. Although supported by the Dutch Reformed Church in South Africa, it was clear to all others, especially the non-White population which suffered under this system, that it was unjust, immoral and sinful. The churches of

English background spoke up against apartheid from the beginning, but were unable to take decisive action against it. These churches, whose members are mostly black, nevertheless include many white people of British descent whose economic interests led them to support apartheid at the polls while condemning it in church resolutions.[7]

There were courageous individuals who opposed the system, such as **Alan Paton** (1903–88), whose novels, beginning with *Cry, the Beloved Country* describe the pain and suffering caused by the system. Deeply Christian, Paton's vision is one of deep compassion for all sides. Paton comes from the British side of the white population. From the Afrikaner side, no one has been better known than **Beyers Naudé** (b. 1915), who suffered rejection by the Dutch Reformed Church and eventually banning (house arrest) by the South African government.

Apartheid lost ground in the days following the release of Nelson Mandela. The laws which codified it in the 1950s were rescinded and the prisoners and exiles came back. Mandela and de Klerk were awarded the Nobel Peace Prize. In this situation of uncertainty, hope and fear, both black and white Christians are praying that their country will develop as a multiracial democracy in which human rights are honoured.

John de Gruchy (b. 1939) gathered an engaging, challenging collection of spiritual writings under the title *Cry Justice!*[8] He was another of the courageous Afrikaners who broke with apartheid. A special characteristic of this daily devotional guide is the inclusion of songs and artwork as well as prayers and meditations from South African Christians. This little book illustrates the wide variety of material which express and shape spirituality, while keeping the social justice dimension in the context of the message of the grace of God.

The book contains the music and words for the powerful hymn, 'Nkosi Sikele' iAfrika', which is sung all over southern Africa. Composed by Enoch Sontonga in the Xhosa language at a Methodist mission school in 1897, it was adopted as the official anthem of the African National Congress in 1912. I have always been deeply moved when I have heard this anthem. Here is an English translation:

> Lord, in your mercy bless Africa
> Lift up the horn of her power and strength.
> In your love and kindness hear our prayer,
> Father look on us, and bless your family.

Come, Spirit come—come and bless us
Come, Spirit come—come and bless us
Father, look down, and bless Africa,
Father look on us, and bless your family.[9]

The most well-known of the Christian opponents of apartheid is **Desmond Tutu** (b. 1931) former Archbishop of Johannesburg and winner of the Nobel Peace Prize. He is the author of a number of short books containing sermons and meditations, appealing for both justice and reconciliation. Tutu is known not only for leading marches and conducting mass funerals for the victims of apartheid, but also for his spiritual leadership. He is known to be a person of prayer, rising very early each morning to spend an hour or more with God. Tutu's passion for social justice in the context of Christian spirituality is expressed in his collection called *An African Prayer Book*, which contains these prayers:

Lord, we thank you that our churches are like big families.
Lord, let your spirit of reconciliation blow over all the earth.
Let Christians live your love. Lord, we praise you in Europe's
    cathedrals, in America's offerings,
And in our African songs of praise.
Lord, we thank you that we have brothers and sisters in all
    the world.
Be with them that make peace.

Amen. (West Africa)

Goodness is stronger than evil;
Love is stronger than hate;
Light is stronger than darkness;
Life is stronger than death;
Victory is ours through Him who loves us. (Desmond Tutu)

God, my father
I am filled
with anguish and puzzlement.
Why, oh God, is there so much
Suffering, such needless suffering?
Everywhere we look there is pain
And suffering.

Why must your people in El Salvador,
In Nicaragua,
In Guatamala,
In ....,
In ....,
Why must there be so much killing,
So much death and destruction,
So much bloodshed,
So much suffering,
So much oppression, and injustice, and poverty, and hunger?...

I am dumbfounded
I am bewildered
And in agony—

In the Eucharist as we offer the bread
That bread is all the bewilderment, the anguish, the blood,
    the pain, the injustice,
The poverty, the hate, the anger, the fear, the death,
The war, the bombs—
And we offer it all together with
The perfect all self-sufficient sacrifice
Of the Lamb without blemish
For peace,
For transfiguration, for compassion,
For Bush, for Hussein, for soldiers,
For civilians, for peace, for Shalom,
For family, for togetherness—

Oh my God, our God, of my Father
When will we ever learn?
When will they ever learn? (Desmond Tutu)[10]

O God, turn your ear to hear me. Protect my children and my cattle, and even if you are weary, please be patient and listen to my prayer. Under the dark cloak of night, the splendour of your world sleeps on, invisible to us. And when your sun moves across the sky each day, I continue to pray to you. May the spirit of our departed ancestors, who can still exercise their influence on us, keep guard over us, from their places beyond the earth. (Nandi, Kenya)[11]

Namibia, which borders South Africa on the northwest, was under the heel of the South African apartheid system until March of 1990. Lutheran Pastor **Zephania Kameeta**, who since independence has been elected a leader in the Namibian Parliament, published a book of prayers in the midst of oppression, *Why, O Lord?* The book introduces the Namibian situation, then includes meditations and paraphrases of Scripture. For example, Psalm 27 begins,

> The Lord is my light and my liberation;
> I will fear no so-called world powers.
> The Lord protects me from all danger;
> I will never be afraid.
> When their 'security forces' attack me
> and try to kill me,
> they stumble and fall.
> Even if their whole imperialist armies surround me,
> I will not be afraid;
> I will still trust in God my Liberator.[12]

These poems give sharp expression to the oppression experienced by black Namibians.

The second main theme in African Christian spirituality is contextualization. What will a Christianity which is fully African look like? The quest for an indigenous cultural expression of Christianity has led to a re-evaluation of the primal religions, and new interest in the ancient African churches of Egypt and Ethiopia, together with careful study of the so-called 'African Independent Churches'.

Missionaries from the North Atlantic countries generally taught Christianity on the basis of their own post-enlightenment, 'modern' assumptions and addressed their answers to the kinds of questions they were accustomed to at home. Christianity became a 'classroom religion' for many people. It taught reading and writing and the correct answers to the questions in the catechism, whether Catholic, Reformed, or Lutheran, but it often did not address the questions Africans raised then and continue to raise, explicitly or implicitly.

Christianity was attractive to Africans because of the prestige of a Scripture, the possibility of confidence in the love of the creator, and the promise of secure and eternal life after death. But post-Enlightenment missionary Christianity did not have much to say about issues of daily concern, the status of the ancestors, the role of spirits and divinities, contact with the unseen world through visions, dreams and animals, and especially matters of health and fertility. These issues had already been secularized in Europe and North America, and missionaries became the agents of secularization in Africa, knowingly or unknowingly.

This contrast became vividly apparent in the ministry of **William Wade Harris** (1865?–1929).[13] A forty-seven-year-old Liberian, Harris was called while in prison to be a prophet. He discarded all western clothing, and set off walking near the Atlantic across Ivory Coast, preaching to indigenous peoples that they should abandon their old gods and be baptized in the name of the Father, Son and Holy Spirit. There had been a few missionaries in Ivory Coast for about twenty years, but they had found little success in convincing people of a 'modern' world-view. Harris, however, spoke to the people within their own world-view. Like them he believed in the power of their gods and spirits and in the possibility of miracles. His demonstration of 'signs and wonders' like those in the Acts of the Apostles convinced many people to burn their old images and amulets and to be baptized by Harris. Unlike the missionaries he did not demand any book learning before baptism. By baptism people felt immediately defended from the revenge of their abandoned gods by the spiritual power of the new God, who loved them. Harris was not concerned about denominations. Some of those baptized by him became Catholic, others Methodist, and still others started indigenous churches. Harris walked all the way to Gold Coast (now Ghana) and back across Ivory Coast to Liberia in the years 1913–15. It is said that over 100,000 people responded to this African prophet, with his bamboo cross, turban and robe, calabash rattle and bowl of baptismal water! He kept the local communities together instead of separating out individual converts as the missionaries did. He also permitted and practised polygamy, a traditional form of African marriage.

The example of the prophet Harris is not unique. Other prophets in Africa in our century also emerged: Garrick Braide in Nigeria, Simon Kimbangu in Zaire, and many others. None of them set out deliberately to 'accommodate' Christianity to African culture, but all of them did an 'end run' around Western ideas of Christianity. In seeking to be faithful to the Bible and to the Spirit, they did produce a form of Christianity which was indigenous to Africa, a 'contextualized' faith. The churches founded by these prophets and others are now looked upon as providing clues for the contextualization of spirituality in the mission-founded churches.

They portend a special type of spirituality which is strange to the European individualist, rationalist spirituality of recent centuries. The major themes are the affirmation of life in this world, as well as beyond the grave, the role of the living dead in the communion of saints, the importance of healing, and the presence of the Spirit to work in power. Some of these themes are found in Pentecostal Christianity on all continents, others are distinctive to Africa.

African Christianity has both gifts and challenges for first-world Christians. I see the gifts as (a) a sense of the presence of God in all things, (b) an experience of the Spirit of God for power to meet the challenges of life, (c) a strong emphasis on the community, and (d) the eagerness to celebrate in music and dance the glory of God. The challenge on the other hand comes from the racially troubled southern region of Africa, where race relations bear some marks of the North American racial atmosphere. It was easy for foreigners to condemn apartheid in South Africa if it did not cost anything to do so; it is much more challenging to change one's own society, so that it will be racially just. Both Native Americans and African Americans have suffered in the United States under European American domination.

Asia

The world's largest continent also has the most people, but the smallest percentage of Christians. Though Christianity began in western Asia, its thought forms seem quite different from those of the ancient civilizations of India and China. On this continent lie some of the most difficult cultural challenges to an indigenous Christian spirituality. As with the other continents, I will not attempt any sort of completeness in this discussion, but select a few highlights.

Japan

No one who has read **Kosuke Koyama**'s (b. 1929) whirlwind theological tour of Asia can assume that Asia has the same cultural similarity as the peoples of Africa. His *Waterbuffalo Theology* hints at the very different situations in Singapore, Thailand, China, Hong Kong, the Philippines, Indonesia, Burma, Vietnam, Japan and Taiwan. In the situation of northern Thailand where he is writing, he speaks of a 'monsoon orientation' as 'cyclical cosmic regularity and its saving dependability without hurry and without argument'.[14] How different from the spirit of the industrialized countries, including his own homeland, Japan! This difference is indicated in the meditations he entitles *Three Mile an Hour God*.[15] Koyama is intensely aware of the cultural differences within Asia as well as those between Asia and the West. His conversational style, freehand drawings, and witty remarks show a down-to-earth spirituality.

Koyama calls for quite a different direction in spirituality from the Latin American and African sources we have discussed. This is not a spirituality of social justice or of contextualization, but a spirituality of the cross, as the place where a God of history expresses wrath about human sin. Koyama is not trying to blend together Asian religions and Christianity, but focusing on the very stumbling block which Paul wrote about: the cross. In his *No Handle on the Cross* Koyama rejects human attempts to control God or to reduce the offensiveness of the Christian message by taking the spotlight off the cross of Jesus. Koyama is very sensitive to the presence of idolatry of various kinds, and writes about it in *Mount Fuji and Mount Sinai*.[16]

Sometimes Koyama sounds very much like Luther's 'theology of the cross' as opposed to a 'theology of glory'. (See Chapter 5 above.) He sounds very much like his compatriot, **Kazoh Kitamori** (b. 1916), author of *Theology of the Pain of God*. Kitamori writes of a mysticism of suffering: 'We become united with the pain of God through our pain, and we are united with God through the joined pains.'[17]

Two earlier twentieth-century Japanese writers round out our discussion of Japanese Christian spirituality. **Kanzo Uchimura** (1861–1929) came from a Samurai family, and became a Christian at school under the influence of Dr William S. Clark. Uchimura joined a group of highly committed and intelligent Christian students. When he returned home, he gave his father a copy of a commentary on Mark which his father threw in the dustbin three times, but Kanzo retrieved it each time. Finally his father was converted to Christianity with the whole family.

Kanzo's student group, however, planning to build a church outside of denominational boundaries, was forced at great sacrifice to refund money given by the Methodist Mission. This event and others turned him away from churches and missionaries. He is best known as the founder of the 'non-church movement', Christianity outside the usual organizations. Yet he did lead a community of Christians, and stated clearly that he was not opposed to the church.

One of his defining moments occurred in the United States. He studied at Amherst College in Massachusetts, where President Seely said to him when he was in great distress, 'Why don't you stop looking inside yourself and look up to Jesus who bore your sin on the cross?' Uchimura wrote on 8 March 1886, 'This was the most important day of my life. The power of Christ's redemption was never so strongly revealed as today. Christ has paid all my debt and can take me back to the purity and holiness which humanity enjoyed before the fall of Adam.'[18]

After returning to Japan, he refused to bow to the emperor's photograph. He was bitterly attacked, became ill, and lost his job. Then began his career as a writer, first of articles and books, then of his own publications, *Tokyo Independent Magazine* and *The Study of the Bible*.

In simplicity Uchimura expressed his love for his homeland and for his saviour: 'I have two J's for me to love. One is Jesus, while the other is Japan. Until today, my life has been encouraged with the enthusiasm to serve these two.'[19]

Another Christian leader from the twentieth century is **Toyohiko Kagawa** (1888–1960). Though he came from an affluent family, he chose to live in the slums of Kobe in order to minister to the poor. On the very first day, he found himself sharing his very small space with a man with a skin disease, who was followed by other homeless persons who moved in with him. Kagawa was not only a social activist, but a poet.

> 'He cannot save Himself'—
> Long ago
> The crowds
> Reviled a Man
> > Who came
> To save them.
> And I,
> Who fain would follow Him,
> Am spent.
> For I can see
> No hope
> For the slums

Because that,
First of all,
   This thing
   Is wrong—
   That men
Should crowd
Thus in the dearth,
   And dark
   And dirt—
Should crowd and throng...

But oh,
The pity, the pity!
My people
Must stay
In the city;
So this six-foot shack
That shelters me
Is the only place
Where I want to be.[20]

He organized labour and peasants' unions to improve their very difficult lot. Kagawa was arrested by the Japanese government several times in the 1940s under suspicion of spreading peace propaganda. World War II seemed to destroy all his work. Yet he reorganized and aided in the rebuilding of Japan, remaining a preacher, even though he was offered high political office. He was devoted not only to evangelizing the Japanese population but to the building of a just society, what he considered the kingdom of God on earth. 'Who will accomplish the successful reconstruction of the economic system, if the Christians do not try to serve in this way? The spirit of brotherhood and love which is at the heart of Christianity is the promise of hope for the new order.'[21]

If a single word were chosen to summarize Kagawa's spirituality it would be love:

Love alone introduces God to me. Love is my sanctuary—in factory, field, city street; in bedroom, office, kitchen, sickroom. I have my sanctuary everywhere I go in the universe. Where Love is, there God is... Love is the ultimate religion. Classify me not by creed: I belong to nothing but Love. Jesus it was who taught that it should be so. Jesus never said that men were to be shunned for their creeds. Love is the ultimate revelation, the final sanctuary.[22]

China

China, the world's largest nation, has a long and varied history of Christian spirituality. The Nestorian Christians established churches from 653 to 845, but then they were totally suppressed under the Tang dynasty. Later, Franciscans and Jesuits visited the royal courts. Among these was Matteo Ricci, discussed above in Chapter 5. It was in the 1800s that Protestants first came to China. Robert Morrison came in 1807, and after years of patient scholarly work, first translated the Bible into Chinese. After 1860, missionary work in China was tainted by the fact that it was forced on the Chinese after two opium wars which were a kind of economic rape. A huge number of foreign missionaries arrived, with good intentions, and built schools, clinics, and churches. All of this was uprooted by the communist movement, starting in the early 1920s with the New Culture movement which was virulently anti-Christian, and finally in the communist takeover in 1949 and the Cultural Revolution of 1966. Christianity was seen as the tool of the capitalist imperialists. Religion in general was seen as superstition, which must be eradicated for the progress of the nation, relying on scientific principles.

So, Chinese Christians have had to face a hostile government almost the entire century, and very many have been imprisoned, tortured, disgraced and killed for their faith. That faith has persisted through the fires of persecution, however, and after the Cultural Revolution ended in 1976 with the death of Mao, the Christians have been able to reorganize and grow at a rapid pace. The communist government has insisted on regulating the Churches, and only allows Protestants who are part of the Three-Self Patriotic Movement (TSPM) to conduct open services and train pastors. Attendance at these open churches in the cities is overwhelming. Meanwhile, Roman Catholics must affiliate with the Catholic Patriotic Association, which seeks to cut all ties to Rome. Others who worship in houses are still persecuted, and must meet in secret. Because of this fact, no one knows the extent of Christianity in China today. Estimates range from 5 to 100 million Christians; perhaps 50 to 60 million is closer to the mark.

These Christians must be very careful about contact with foreign Christians. They are in fact proving that Chinese Christianity is indigenous to China, and not dependent on the West. They have survived the most harsh persecution, and thereby have left behind all that is not essential to Christian spirituality: church buildings, church institutions, public acceptance. These all went during the Cultural Revolution.

What is essential did remain and grow, apart from any support from foreigners: the Bible, the community, the family. What is it that has continued to attract Chinese people to faith in Jesus Christ? Many of them say that it is joy. Though public preaching is not permitted, new Christians say that they have observed a joy in the life of Christians which contrasts with the bleak joylessness of the communist ideology.

The Chinese example is a challenge to affluent Christians elsewhere in the world. They have followed a spirituality of the cross: suffering, endurance, patience, poverty. In the course of their trauma, they have left behind Western denominations. A North American interprets this challenge as follows:

> There may be elements in our culture—its commercialism, consumerism, greed, and hedonistic values—that are also alien to Christianity, but the threat is more subtle and difficult to handle. In our interpretation of Christianity it is so terribly important to make the distinction between what is 'Christian' and what is 'culture'. This may not always be possible, but the attempt must be made. Christianity must not be made a captive to any culture—East or West, capitalist or communist.[23]

On the other hand, the Chinese example raises the question of the importance for Christians of contact with others of the faith throughout the world. A temporary isolation may be necessary because of critics in the Chinese government, but Christian spirituality does need encouragement and interchange with an ecumenical, world-wide community.

India

In India, we see a development outwardly similar to African context-ualization, but quite different in content. The development of a friendly Christian relationship to Hinduism goes in the direction of a mysticism not characteristic of Africa. Drawing on the resources of Ramanuja, Sadhu Sundar Singh and Krishna Pillai, **A.J. Appasamy** (1891– 1975) developed a Christian spirituality in the *bhakti* tradition of Hinduism. Bhakti refers to the way of salvation by devotion rather than by the other two major paths in Hinduism: knowledge or moral achievement. It is the path that seems to be the closest to the Christian concept of salvation by grace. Starting from his doctoral dissertation at Oxford, Appasamy related the message of the Gospel of John to Indian mysticism. He was sympathetic to the use of Hindu terminology and practice.

I must also mention the Albanian nun who has become known world wide for her work among the sick and dying in Calcutta. **Mother Teresa** (b. 1910) no longer belongs to any particular continent, as the work of her order now circles the globe. Her spirituality is simple and biblical: she sees Christ in the suffering persons she helps.[24] She insists that her sisters take their prayer and worship lives very seriously, or they will burn out in serving the poorest of the poor. This profound simplicity has become a witness to Christians and non-Christians alike. Mother Teresa has combined a fearless confrontation with traditional customs and government authorities with a savvy ability to get things done. Yet she attends daily Mass as an essential part of her day.

We cannot all be Mother Teresas, yet the holism of her spirituality is worthy of emulation: prayer and work go together.

Other developments in Asia include the impressive growth of Christianity among the Batak peoples of Indonesia, the Minjung theology of Korea, the Christian dialogue with Buddhism in Japan, and the quests for indigenization in the southern islands such as Papua New Guinea.

Australasia and the South Pacific

The Christian faith came to this part of the world only after the explorations of the late 1700s. Indigenous populations responded to missionaries in the 1800s, and European settlers brought a mixture of attitudes to Christian spirituality.

Let us begin with Australia itself, named by a Portuguese explorer, Pedro de Quiros, who searched for 'Austrialia [sic] del Espiritu Santo' (south land of the Holy Spirit) but never found it. This continent is home to an indigenous population now known as Aborigines. Their own spiritual practice, stemming from a history estimated at 40,000 years, focuses on a Dream Time and on harmony with the earth. When Europeans started arriving with the First Fleet of prisoners, the Aboriginal peoples were not regarded as fully human. Missionaries were slow to take an interest in them, but when they did, they showed the familiar assumption that Christianity and Western culture were indissoluble. The Aboriginal culture was so different from the Westerners that basic assumptions were often never understood between them. In the end, although they were paternalistic and often destructive to Aboriginal culture, the missionaries may have provided for the survival of Aboriginal people. They alone defended them against greedy frontier settlers and industrialists who would have liked to see them disappear off the face of the earth. Exactly that happened to the people of Tasmania, the island just off the south coast. Today as with indigenous peoples elsewhere, there is population increase among the Aborigines, and a new appreciation of their culture both by their own leaders and by the European Australians. Among the developments is a growing Christian fellowship among Aborigines which is led and extended by Aborigines themselves.

It may even affect other Christian Australians, as they reconsider their spirituality. Consider this remark by Guboo Ted Thomas, sole elder of the Yuin people.

> We are truly part of this land—it is Mother Earth to us. We do not own it; the land owns us... There are too many churchgoers and not enough Christians. There needs to be a revival among the whites so they can break through the old barriers, so they can walk more closely with the Aboriginal people. This is part of my work—not only to stop the bulldozers, but also to take white folk into a Renewing of the Dreaming ceremony at Wallage Lakes. In spring and summer over a hundred whites come to participate in this revival at the lakes and in the mountains. I try to show them that we are part of the trees, part of the bush, part of everything, and it is wonderful, because this is what so many whites are searching for in Australia. This wholeness and this walking together is exactly the same thing we find in the Bible.[25]

This suggests to me that Christians can gain from an appreciation of the land itself; renewal is possible not just from books, but from the open landscape.

Today's Aboriginal Christian is not the cultural copy of the European, but the critical adapter of what is fitting to Aboriginal culture.

In an exciting process of inculturation, they are successfully integrating the Christian gospel into Aboriginal culture and traditional belief systems. So the worship of Aboriginal communities has a refreshing internal integrity, and sits easily to a wide spectrum of Christian tradition. Ecumenism comes naturally to Aborigines.

Aboriginal theologians are proclaiming a God who has lived with them throughout their history, who gave them the Dreaming, and spoke to them through it. Aboriginal artists are conveying Christian truths through traditional media and traditional art forms. And together they are offering their insights and the deep spirituality of their race as a generous gift towards the healing of the materialism and cynicism of so many white Australians.[26]

Rose Kunoth-Monks, an Aboriginal Christian, after describing her experiences, concludes as follows.

To sum up, then, it appears that what happened in the religious area was this: The Christian faith was readily accepted because it was seen to address itself to a felt need. However the Aboriginal Christians discriminated between what they saw as the central tenets of the Christian faith and the Western application of that faith to their specific cultural situation. The latter they did not accept.[27]

Today Australia is a nation of over 18 million people, 70 per cent of whom live in the ten main cities. About 73 per cent claim to be Christians.

The history of the European Australians, beginning with convicts in the First Fleet of 1788, is marked by growing self-respect and toleration of differences. The Anglo and Irish populations have long been in tension, reflected in a lack of cooperation between Catholics and Anglicans. But today, these two largest churches in Australia are working together.

Christianity did not have an auspicious beginning in Australia. Richard Johnson, the chaplain of First Fleet was also a magistrate, and thus the church was thoroughly part of the penal system. His first church, built at his own expense in 1793, was burned by arson in 1798, indicating poignantly the Australian resistance to imposed religion! Later, Samuel Marsden, known as 'the flogging parson' for a similar combination of roles, set back relations between Protestant and Roman Catholic, as he put down Irish rebellions.

As in many countries, individual members of the church often bring greater credit to Christianity than do the churches as a whole. Two outstanding Australian Christians who helped the nation as a whole were **Caroline Chisholm** (1808–77) and **John Flynn** (1880–1951). Chisholm, known as 'the emigrant's friend', was appalled at the condition of women and families who arrived in Australia among a population of men without funds or savvy. She founded an emigrants society which provided both to the groups of emigrants which she encouraged to come. Her Roman Catholic faith led her to modify her life plan to spend her energies for people in need. Caroline Chisholm even appeared on the Australian five dollar note!

John Flynn, a Presbyterian, affected the outback of Australia. After observing the desolation of frontier life and the need for basic spiritual guidance for individuals who were often a hundred miles from the nearest human being, he wrote the 'Bushman's Companion'. This little handbook included a funeral service, hymns, Bible passages and first aid. In the 1920s he stubbornly persisted against many obstacles to develop the 'pedal wireless' to give radio contact and a system of flying doctors, who would attend the sick far from any town, through the Australian Inland Mission. His motto, 'For Christ and the Continent' is now the motto of Frontier Services. His achievement was to make the outback livable for families.

A story of women's persistence in the face of male opposition is that of the Roman Catholic Sisters of St Joseph ('Josephites') founded in Adelaide in 1867. Although they staffed the expanding system of Catholic parochial schools and were respected by the poor for their own simple lifestyle, they were opposed by bishops who wanted to control them. They escaped their control in 1888.

True to their denominational heritages, the Methodists and the Salvation Army have gained respect in Australia for their work in the inner cities. Because of positions on temperance, gambling and the sabbath, however, they and other denominations suffer the reputation of being 'wowsers', pious people who do not allow others to have a good time— 'killjoys'.

Christian spirituality in Australia has suffered from connections with state control, from deep prejudices among denominations, from the negative images of women produced by its unbalanced population in early decades, and from white rejection of other races. But these problems, though not ended, are being confronted by people with strong spiritual commitments today.

New Zealand, Australia's neighbour to the southeast, has both similarities and differences from Australia. Its indigenous population, the Maoris, did not arrive until the fourteenth century AD, and were quite different from the Aborigines. They were renowned as fierce warriors who ate their enemies, even consuming the crew of a British ship in 1809, in revenge for the flogging of a chieftain. But they were also very curious about Western culture and encouraged missionaries. First under the direction of Samuel Marsden, who seemed to leave a much more positive story in New Zealand than he had in Australia, the missionaries found a receptive hearing. It was only in the later 1800s that Christianity came to be accepted on a deeper level among Maoris. Ringatu and Ratana movements, among others, were attempts to draw all Maoris together from 500 tribes to oppose the settlement of the land by Pakehas (Europeans). Churches by these names continue to attract some Maoris, but most are members of traditional denominations. Maoritanga, the Maori cultural traditions, have been integrated more into the nation's spirituality than in many other settlement countries. The Anglican Prayer Book includes language and prayers from the Maori tradition.

As in Australia, the Anglican Church is strong in New Zealand, along with Roman Catholics, Presbyterians, Methodists and others. But it seems there is relatively little racial discrimination in New Zealand between the indigenous and colonial populations.

It has been suggested that rugby is the national religion of New Zealand, though the percentage of Christians is very high. Surely the sport shows the dedication and interest of large numbers of people, and demonstrates that spirituality is not merely abstract argument or habitual ritual. Passions run deep for what matters to people's personal lives.

The islands of the Pacific are commonly called Oceania. This includes some 25,000 islands including Melanesia, Micronesia and Polynesia. It may be surprising to learn that Oceania is one of the most Christianized areas of the world. Large parts of island populations are Christian, often more than 90 per cent. The islanders have a spirituality which is a blend of their indigenous traditions, Western Christianity and the awareness of the wide ocean around them. Many include a serious social justice concern about nuclear arms and testing. Christians on these islands have protested the use of their area by the great powers for nuclear testing and dumping.

Europe

The continent seen to be most Christian in previous centuries has had a difficult time in the twentieth century. The optimism of the first decade was shattered by World War I; the Depression of the 1930s and World War II devastated the continent. The horrors of the Holocaust, the growth of Marxist atheism, secularism and many intellectual challenges to the truth of Christianity have left a continent nominally Christian, with only a remnant serious about Christian spirituality. Yet that remnant has been both innovative and devoted to the study of the tradition.

Among the many twentieth-century writers on mysticism, perhaps the most influential in the English-speaking world was **Evelyn Underhill** (1875–1941). She became a mystic in the philosophical, Platonic sense before being baptized as a Christian in adulthood. The person who influenced her most became her spiritual director: Baron Friedrich von Hugel. He was a modernist Roman Catholic lay theologian living in England.

She is known for her major study, *Mysticism*, first published in 1911, and her later *Worship* of 1936. She drew the attention of many people to the classical mystical texts. She devoted herself to a ministry of personal spiritual direction from her home. Retreats were also a special interest. So Underhill's interest in spirituality and mysticism were not merely academic. She was actively involved with the practical problems of real people.

On the continent, one of the outstanding Christian theologians and martyrs was **Dietrich Bonhoeffer** (1906–45). He first became widely known for his provocative commentary on the Sermon on the Mount, *The Cost of Discipleship*. Like Kierkegaard almost a century earlier, he castigated his own Lutheran tradition for preaching 'cheap grace', an easy, uninvolved Christianity. The whole nation, he said, has been baptized with little sense of the meaning of being Jesus' disciple.

Later Bonhoeffer became known as a martyr, after his execution by the Nazis five days before the Americans liberated his prison. He had been arrested for his role in plotting the assassination of Hitler. Once he had been safe in New York, but felt he had to return to Germany to fight Hitler. While he was there he taught at a secret seminary, in Finkenwalde, where he gave spiritual direction to the students and wrote *Life Together*, which describes the basis of Christian community. It also describes his advice for reading Scripture and meditation.

Some have come to know Bonhoeffer exclusively through *Letters and Papers from Prison*, published after his death by his friend Eberhard Bethge. The letters introduced phrases much used in 1960s theology: 'religionless Christianity', 'secular holiness' and 'man come of age'. He was critical of 'religion' as a replacement for the living God, and decried the 'God of the gaps', a God who was only used to explain what science did not yet explain. Some people took his book as the banner of a politicized Christianity, leaving out traditional spirituality altogether. Since that time, more balance has come in the interpretation of Bonhoeffer, and he may well be one of the theologians and spiritual writers who is remembered into the next century.

In the Orthodox world, the twentieth century has seen great suffering under the Bolshevik regimes, especially that of Stalin. But there is a new freedom for spiritual pursuits as the Soviet Empire disintegrates at the end of the century. The revival of what is old has marked the Orthodox tradition again and again through the centuries. In the twentieth century, hesychasm, the *Philokalia*, *The Way of a Pilgrim*, and movements among the Russian intellectuals have again revived what is old. Beyond the Eastern European countries where Orthodoxy is strong, there has been impressive growth in western Europe and North America, where émigrés have come to live, pray and study. The translation into English of Orthodox works is having significant impact on Catholics and Protestants. The Anglican community, especially, has seen its calling as a bridge between East and West.

North America

Finally we come to the author's own continent, where many have experienced great gains in material prosperity in this century, and in spite of participating in many wars, have not suffered from them on their own ground. Yet the inequalities in the societies of Canada and the USA and the continuing hunger for genuine spiritual nourishment are very real.

One of the outstanding figures in Christian spirituality of our century was **Thomas Merton** (1915–68). He was born in France of parents from New Zealand and the USA. His childhood was spent mostly in Europe, where he mastered several languages. By the time he entered Columbia University in New York he was already writing a great deal. His conversion to Catholicism and quick entrance into a monastery were shocking to some of his friends, but somewhat parallel to the changes in Augustine's life 1,500 years earlier. Like Augustine's *Confessions*, Merton's *Seven Storey Mountain* told his inner autobiography. Merton's book became a best seller and made his name well-known in the Christian world.

Merton entered the Trappist monastery of Our Lady of Gethsemani, Kentucky, in 1941. The Trappists are one of the strictest branches of Catholic monks. They continue to practise the full seven traditional prayer times each day, and to follow a vow of silence, not speaking to each other except for limited occasions. It was a life following the Benedictine Rule, with manual labour, prayer and sacred reading. The success of Merton's autobiography and subsequent books eventually produced the major part of the monastery's income.

Merton loved the contemplative life, but he also hated certain aspects of it. He was in friction with the abbot over the rules of enclosure and how to deal with his writings. But he would not have developed into the writer he did without the monastic life. He was told to write about early Cistercian saints and translate their writings. This led him to become an expert on monastic history, not only of his own order, but of all monasticism going back to the Egyptian hermits.

Eventually Merton himself wanted the solitude of the hermit. After a long period of requests, the order agreed to approve the practice of hermitage for some stable monks, and Merton was given permission. He had his own house, called Our Lady of Carmel.

Early in his career, Merton had been enthusiastic about the writings of John of the Cross and Teresa of Avila. Later he came to love Mother Julian of Norwich even more.

His interest in Asian religion was roused in the 1960s, and he explored the relations between Christian and Buddhist meditation. He died tragically in an electrical accident at a conference in Bangkok, in 1968.

Merton brought a renewal of monastic life not only to his monastery and his order, but also to seekers everywhere. He did not really break new ground, but revived the old, applying it to new problems. He stands as a witness for the contemplative life as a genuine Christian calling, without any 'social utility'. He believed a life of contemplative prayer was worthwhile without any social works to justify it. But he was very much interested in social problems, and a strong advocate for peace.

In later life he was also a witness for Christians to enter into dialogue with people of other faiths. He did not leave Christianity behind, but explored what Buddhists and Christians could learn from each other.

A similar question is being raised by many North Americans about the relation of Christianity to Native cultures and religions. Many American Indians and a number of non-Indians are thinking deeply about the relationship between Christianity and the religions of Native peoples. Many are asking if the commonalities of these two have been overlooked. Others are calling for a Native spirituality within Christianity. Especially attractive is the traditional Indian reverence for 'all my relatives' (all living creatures and even all things in nature) and the honoured roles for women in these religions. Many Native Americans are Christian and are seeking a spirituality which will combine their traditions with the gospel of Jesus.

The African American population is overwhelmingly Christian, and has been nourished down through the centuries by a spirituality of endurance, liberation and celebration. African Americans have suffered unspeakably from slavery and then discrimination. Those sufferings have produced a community drawn together in worship which reaches the heart. James Cone, who earlier wrote hard-hitting books of black liberation theology, has turned in recent years to an analysis of the spirituality of the black church. He sees in the music and preaching of the Christian community the core of values which has sustained African Americans.

Martin Luther King, Jr (1926–68) is the best known of African Americans throughout the world. It is no accident that the civil rights leader was also a Baptist preacher. His vision of the mountain the night before his death testifies to spiritual roots which sustained his quest for justice through militant non-violence. His *Letter from a Birmingham Jail*, explaining why he chose to break the law for the sake of justice, and *Strength to Love*, indicating the spiritual basis for a long-term struggle, both testify to a spirituality which was expressed in his public actions.

As we approach the end of the century, there are four developments in American spirituality which call for special comment: (1) the influence of psychology, (2) women's spirituality, (3) twelve-step spirituality and (4) creation-centred spirituality.

(1) The world of thought in which spirituality has developed in North America has been deeply influenced by the relatively new discipline of psychology. Perhaps more than any other nation, Americans seek self-fulfilment, self-realization and mental health through their spiritualities. This point underlies all three of the movements on this list, but many others.

On the one hand, I see this as a positive 'contextualizing' of the gospel in America. Christians seek to meet people where they are hurting. The theme of healing is a very important one to many of us as we think of Christian spirituality. The charismatic Catholic Francis MacNutt has written helpful works on this theme, as well as the trio, Matt and Dennis Linn and Sheila Fabricant Linn. Morton Kelsey, an Episcopalian has written prolifically on healing, dreams, speaking in tongues and other themes. All of them include 'inner healing' of emotional wounds from childhood. This is a new kind of approach in the history of Christian spirituality which has been influenced by the psychologists. It is a very helpful approach, in my opinion.

A number of major writers on spirituality base their understanding of the human mind on that of Karl Jung. Jung was much more friendly to Christianity than was Freud, but others think that his viewpoint distorts the Christian message, and that Freud or someone more recent would be a better basis.

But on the other hand, the influence of psychology has been limiting. It can produce a self-absorption which is blind to social justice and ecological balance. If all I want is mental health, I will seek what I can get out of Christian spirituality, but I will not have it in balance. If we listen to the Latin Americans, the Africans, the Asians, we can be encouraged to see the power of God in healing individuals, but we will not be allowed to stop there. Our neighbours will force us to consider all four of the dimensions of spirituality and not just be absorbed in ourselves.

(2) The churches of the West are in the midst of a serious re-evaluation of their spiritual roots in response to the new consciousness among women. In the USA, the radical feminism of the few in the 1970s has developed into a more widespread women's movement in the churches which is influencing not just personnel policies and the language of hymns, but also the way we think about God. Women's Christian spirituality has become a major concern.

Much of the history of Christian spirituality, with some notable exceptions, has been developed and reported by men. The question that is being asked is whether a thoroughgoing change in tone is needed so that the concerns of women are also addressed. Among these are the way in which Christians image God. If God is uniformly referred to with male metaphors such as Father, Lord and King, and the male pronoun is always used, then it is difficult to see how women are made in the image of God. The biblical and historical witness to a variety of images for God has many times been lost in popular piety, leaving many women alienated.

Another concern is the view of the body and sexuality in Christian spirituality. The tradition has had large numbers of celibate men as leading teachers. These men did not have a balanced view of the goodness of sex as God's creation. Women appeared to them as temptations to sin. Even non-celibate men have looked upon women more as sex objects, and therefore temptresses, than as partners in the spiritual life.

A fresh view of the relation of the sexes in spirituality is emerging, in which the female as well as male character of God is recognized, and the gifts of women are recognized along with those of men. The experiences and views of men should not be the norm; women's views and experiences are fully as important.

Two kinds of writers of women's spirituality have emerged. One type wishes to remain within the Christian tradition, reforming it to avoid dualisms and hierarchies, and to value highly experience, especially the experiences of women, including women from other cultures. This means reading the Bible with different eyes, looking for the women, asking how it looked from their point of view. It also means being sceptical of the Christian tradition as a whole, looking for obvious and not so obvious ways in which males have undermined Paul's assertion that in Christ Jesus 'there is neither male nor female'.[28]

A second kind of women's spirituality has left Christianity behind. Finding the Bible and the theological tradition of the churches just too patriarchal, a number of women have started their own spiritual groups. Some of them worship the Mother Goddess of older religions, some practise a modern revision of witchcraft, but others simply look for healing ideas, including New Age materials.

(3) A dialogue between twelve-step programmes and Christian spirituality is underway. Alcoholics Anonymous was founded in the USA in the 1930s by two men, 'Bill W. and Dr Bob' (William Wilson (1895–1971) and Robert Smith (1879–1950)), who were deeply influenced by the Oxford Group, later known as Moral Rearmament.[29] A thorough discussion of the influences which shaped AA indicates both Christian and secular movements.[30] They and other alcoholics were often turned off by the churches and conventional Christianity, but they deeply believed in the message of the gospel. They developed groups for alcoholics which accepted all people as the churches never did. Here are the twelve steps which they developed based in part on the eight principles of the Oxford Group:

1. We admitted we were powerless over alcohol, that our lives had become unmanageable.

2. Came to believe that a Power greater than ourselves could restore us to sanity.

3. Made a decision to turn our will and our lives over to the care of God *as we understood Him*.

4. Made a searching and fearless moral inventory of ourselves.

5. Admitted to God, to ourselves, and to another human being the exact nature of our wrongs.

6. Were entirely ready to have God remove all these defects of character.

7. Humbly asked Him to remove our shortcomings.

8. Made a list of all persons we had harmed, and became willing to make amends to them all.

9. Made direct amends to such people wherever possible, except when to do so would injure them or others.

10. Continued to take personal inventory and when we were wrong promptly admitted it.

11. Sought through prayer and meditation to improve our conscious contact with God *as we understand Him*, praying only for knowledge of His will for us and the power to carry that out.

12. Having had a spiritual awakening as the result of these steps, we tried to carry this message to alcoholics and to practice these principles in all our affairs.[31]

These steps obviously include wisdom from the tradition of Christian spirituality. Some have found these steps in the Bible as a whole[32] or in the Beatitudes from the Sermon on the Mount.[33] Nevertheless, the authors felt it necessary to expand the concept of God into what is commonly called one's 'Higher Power', since many alcoholics could not relate to the usual picture of God.

Eventually over the years, the original twelve steps have been supplemented by a literature incorporating basic attitudes, prayer and meditation. One of the most widely used texts in the spirituality of AA is the 'Serenity Prayer' which is the first part of a longer prayer composed by theologian Reinhold Niebuhr:

God grant me the grace to accept with serenity the things
    I cannot change,
courage to change the things I can, and wisdom to know
    the difference,
living one day at a time, enjoying one moment at a time;
accepting hardship as the pathway to peace,
taking as you did this sinful world as it is, not as I would
    have it;
trusting that you will make all things right, if I surrender
    to your will;
that I may be reasonably happy in this life,
and supremely happy with you forever in the next.

Amen.[34]

In recent decades this literature has increasingly caught the attention of Christian spiritual directors and pastors. Perhaps there is some possibility of more cooperation between the churches and AA.

One of the elements in this interest is the insight about the ubiquitous nature of addiction.[35] That is, what AA pioneered for one kind of addiction is relevant for others, and not only the obvious ones such as drugs, gambling and overeating. It turns out that the compulsive behaviours we find in ourselves we do not consciously choose; they relate to Paul's lament in Romans, 'Instead of doing the good things I want to do, I carry out the sinful things I do not want.'[36]

The twelve steps are a programme which includes several features of earlier spirituality, such as a soul friend, daily examen, restitution, surrender to God, sharing your belief with others. It focuses on the discovery and overcoming of irrational, harmful habits which have at their root the insistence that 'I am God'. The root of addiction is seen to be spiritual, and healing begins by surrender to grace, the gift of God.

The combination of the twelve steps, the regular group meetings, and the personal mentor provide a powerful programme for spiritual change, one that I think is of great potential value for church members.

(4) Finally I would like to discuss 'creation-centred spirituality', as developed by **Matthew Fox** (b. 1940). He is a former Dominican priest with a doctorate in spirituality who has developed both a centre for developing and practising his insights and a series of books. He knows the

history of Christian spirituality very well, and has developed a sharp critique of it. Fox distinguishes between the creation theme and the fall–redemption theme in Christianity. He judges that only the first is valid, and on it he bases his teaching. The fourteen themes of creation spirituality as he summarizes it include the creative Word of God, original blessing (instead of original sin), the celebration of all beings, the unknown, unnameable God who is a non-God, the divinization and deification of humanity, spirituality as a spiral growth process, compassion and justice, Jesus as a reminder of what it means to be God's child, and finally laughter, newness and joy, an affirmation of pleasure.[37] Further, he affirms panentheism, the view that all things are in God, and realized eschatology, which he defines as eternal life beginning now.

'We have often been fed introverted, anti-artistic, anti-intellectual, apolitical, sentimental, dualistic, ascetic and in many ways masochistic spirituality parading as Christian spirituality.'[38] He sees these things in the fall–redemption spirituality which he distinguishes from creation spirituality. He is especially critical of Augustine and the classic reformers, Luther and Calvin.

On the other hand he especially loves Meister Eckhart (see Chapter 4 above), and finds creation spirituality also in Benedict, Pelagius, Hildegard, Francis, Thomas, Mechthild, Julian, John of the Cross, George Fox, Rosemary Reuther and Jon Sobrino.[39]

Fox's spirituality has many features that are attractive to me. He takes the Christian tradition seriously, yet uses his own criteria to distinguish the wheat from the chaff. He uses his knowledge of the tradition to critique the tradition. He takes seriously the ecological and political dimensions of spirituality. His insights into the creative process are refreshing, and his affirmation of pleasure is needed.

Yet, it seems that he has thrown out a vital part of Christian spirituality by discarding the fall–redemption theme. How can he separate creation and redemption so absolutely? These are themes that belong together. It is a central point of Christian praise and spiritual energy that God has forgiven our sin through the death and resurrection of Jesus. Fox seems to reject the very centre of Christian belief in his version of creation spirituality.

As we come to the close of the twentieth century, there are many types of spirituality available. Some of them ignore the Christian tradition, others seek to develop it. The wise person will weigh carefully the biblical message and the tradition in making choices, but will be open to new perspectives from other continents as well as recent writers. Among many such writers, too numerous to mention here, Henry Nouwen and Richard Foster have been very accessible and helpful to me. Neither one has founded a 'school', but both draw selectively on the Christian tradition to make contemporary observations which reach the heart.

Recommended Reading

General

A.M. Allchin, *The Kingdom of Love and Knowledge: The Encounter between Orthodoxy and the West*, New York: Seabury, 1982.

Robert McAfee Brown, *Spirituality and Liberation: Overcoming the Great Fallacy*, Louisville: Westminster, 1988.

Charles Cummings, *Eco-Spirituality: Toward a Reverent Life*, New York: Paulist Press, 1991.

Vincent J. Donovan, *Christianity Rediscovered: An Epistle from the Masai*, SCM Press, 1992.

William Dyrness, *Learning about Theology from the Third World*, Grand Rapids, Michigan: Zondervan, 1990.

Duncan Ferguson, editor, *New Age Spirituality: An Assessment*, Louisville, Kentucky: Westminster/John Knox, 1993.

Gustavo Gutierrez, *We Drink From Our Own Wells: The Spiritual Journey of a People*, SCM Press, 1991.

Bukole Wa Ilunga, *Paths of Liberation: A Third World Spirituality*, Maryknoll, New York: Orbis, 1984.

Kosuke Koyama, *Mount Fuji and Mount Sinai: Pilgrimage in Theology*, SCM Press, 1988.

Kosuke Koyama, *Three Mile an Hour God*, SCM Press 1979.

Kosuke Koyama, *Waterbuffalo Theology*, SCM Press, 1974.

Gerald G. May, *Addiction and Grace*, San Francisco: Harper, 1988.

Marie Augusta Neal, SND deN, *A Socio-Theology of Letting Go: The Role of a First World Church Facing Third World Peoples*, New York: Paulist, 1977.

Susan Rakoczy, editor, *Common Journey, Different Paths: Spiritual Direction in Cross Cultural Perspective*, Maryknoll, New York: Orbis, 1995.

Aylward Shorter, *African Christian Spirituality*, New York: Macmillan, 1978.

John H. Timmerman, *Sexuality and Spiritual Growth*, New York: Crossroad, 1992.

Evelyn Underhill, *Mysticism: A Study in the Nature and Development of Man's Spiritual Consciousness*, One World Publishers, 1993.

Japan

Norimichi Ebizawa, editor, *Japanese Witnesses for Christ*, World Christian Books. New York: Association Press, 1957.

Toyochiko Kagawa, *Jesus Through Japanese Eyes: A Study of the Daily Life of Jesus*, Lutterworth Press, 1934.

Toyochiko Kagawa, *Meditations*, Greenwood Press, 1994.

Kazoh Kitamori, *Theology of the Pain of God*, Richmond, Virginia: John Knox Press, 1958.

Jesse M. Trout, *Kagawa, Japanese Prophet*, World Christian Books, New York: Association Press, 1959.

Australasia

Leonora Mosende Douglas, editor, *World Christianity: Oceania*, Monrovia, California: MARC, 1986.

John Garrett, *To Live among the Stars: Christian Origins in Oceania*, Geneva: WCC Publications, 1982.

Hans Mol, *The Faith of Australians*, Sydney: George Allen and Unwin, 1985.

Hans Mol, *The Firm and the Formless: Religion and Identity in Aboriginal Australia*, Waterloo, Ontario: Wilfrid Laurier University Press, 1982.

Hans Mol, *The Fixed and the Fickle: Religion and Identity in New Zealand*, Waterloo, Ontario: Wilfrid Laurier University Press, 1982.

Hans Mol, *Religion in Australia: A Sociological Investigation*, Melbourne: Thomas Nelson, 1971.

Muriel Porter, *Land of the Spirit? The Australian Religious Experience*, Geneva: Risk Book series, WCC Publications, 1990.

Roger C. Thompson, *Religion in Australia: A History*, Melbourne: Oxford University Press, 1995.

G.W. Tromph, editor, *The Gospel is not Western: Black Theologies from the Southwest Pacific*, Maryknoll, New York: Orbis, 1987.

China

G. Thompson Brown, *Christianity in the People's Republic of China*, Atlanta: John Knox, 1983.

Jonathan Chao, *The China Mission Handbook: A Portrait of China and its Church*, Hong Kong: Chinese Church Research Centre, 1989.

Raymond Fung, compiler and translator, *Households of God on China's Soil*, Geneva: World Council of Churches, 1982.

Paul E. Kauffman, *China: The Emerging Challenge: A Christian Perspective*, Grand Rapids, Michigan: Baker, 1982.

Where Do We Go from Here?

There are many ways of analysing the story I have just told. It is an incomplete story, unwieldy, with rough edges. Each of us will draw our own conclusions. The basic premise of this overview is that we who live today are in continuity with the past and with others throughout the world. There are no 'good old days' in the sense of sentimental longing for a perfect time. Rather, the story goes on with ever new challenges and hopes. We have the privilege of knowing the story better than any previous generation. How we understand it, however, is not automatic and easy.

We look back over the story

Christian spirituality is a style of walking in the Holy Spirit. It therefore involves the whole of life, not some private segment. It is the way we relate to God, to ourselves, to others and to the creation, and their relation to us. The Bible gives a potpourri of normative principles, positive and negative examples of life experience, and the gospel of Jesus Christ on which all else depends.

The early centuries of Christianity were characterized by an expansion to many cultures, Asian, African and European. Within the Roman Empire and in other places, severe persecutions marked Christianity from the beginning. The Jewish affirmation of creation was frequently dimmed and sometimes lost, leaving a legacy of denigration of the body, sexuality and women in the tradition. The spiritual and moral disciplines of the faith were emphasized by many writers, as well as the growth of mystical communion or union with God.

The Eastern part of the Roman Empire, later called Byzantine, developed in different ways from the West, with an emphasis on the resurrection as victory over death and the theosis (or divinization) of humans, rather than the focus on sin and forgiveness as in the West. The icon and the Jesus Prayer, in the context of the divine liturgy with its Eucharist, came to characterize Eastern spirituality, which has constantly renewed itself by going back to the tradition.

Monasticism in the West was a lay protest movement which engendered much Roman Catholic spiritual writing. The ideals of the orders expanded into service for the world with the mendicant orders of the thirteenth century and the Jesuits in the sixteenth. The 'love of learning and the desire for God' were developed in the monasteries.

Protestants emerged to challenge the whole Catholic structure, including its assumptions about spirituality. Their main point was 'grace alone, faith alone, Scripture alone'. Protestants started afresh, with various degrees of borrowing from Catholic spirituality, but always rooted in their understanding of biblical teaching.

The modern age was a time for throwing off the 'superstitions' of both Catholics and Protestants, or at least fitting them into a new understanding of the role of reason. The traditions developed puritanism, pietism, evangelicalism on the Protestant side, as well as the maverick Kierkegaard. The Catholics centred into personal spirituality, especially the French school, preceded by a maverick, Pascal. During this time Christianity began to spread to continents other than Europe, but the non-European contributions to the church universal were not usually appreciated.

The twentieth century has seen the development of Christian faith on a global scale, in some sense fulfilling the promise of the first centuries. It is time now for Christians in Europe and North America to listen not only to the writers of the past, but also to peoples of the present from different cultural traditions. This includes peoples of other continents as well as Native Americans and African Americans. The role of women in the historical development of Christianity and in the present has been seriously neglected; the male-dominated tradition has a great deal to learn from women. We can hope for a future of mutual understanding and cooperation, though that will not happen without painful struggles towards reconciliation.

The root metaphors of spirituality

A number of ways have been used to classify types of spirituality. One of these is to place them on a graph, in which kataphatic and apophatic are at the left and right, and the heart and mind are at the top and bottom.[1] Such a chart can be helpful in identifying psychological tendencies in persons or schools of thought. Another helpful method for people with theological training is that of Geoffrey Wainwright, who connects H. Richard Niebuhr's well-known typology from *Christ and Culture* to spirituality.[2]

Here I will not attempt to classify all types of Christian spirituality, but to illumine certain metaphors which dominate some of the writers and schools of spirituality discussed above.

In an attempt to understand our lives we use fundamental images, or root metaphors. Each image has value but none is adequate by itself. For example, the Bible pictures God as rock, light and fortress; lion, bear and eagle; king, father and shepherd; mother, lover and friend. None of these is adequate for the nature of God, as Pseudo-Dionysius would remind us. The same is true of our pictures of the Christian life.

The basis of Christian life may be pictured as *rescue, redemption* or *justification*. 'Jesus saves' means most simply that Jesus rescues the sinner from the powers greater than any person: sin and death. Redemption means setting free a slave by purchase. Justification takes place in the courtroom: the guilty one is declared innocent on the basis of another's interceding. All of these metaphors have in common the initiative of God, who loves and frees us from internal and external powers which bind us. Some might argue that these images refer only to the inception of the Christian life, but on the contrary, the most experienced and mature saints have clung to them. Whatever role our efforts play in Christian living, these metaphors imply that the fundamental fact is that we remain in need all our lives, and rely on God's love to save, redeem, liberate, justify. The spiritualities of the Lutheran and Reformed traditions place these metaphors in the centre.

Another set of images suggests the process of Christian living. *Growth, unification* and *healing* all describe gradual changes. Biological growth in plants and animals is taken as a model of maturing in the Christian walk. Another view is that we are divided as selves, and the Christian life is a matter of being put back together again, both in terms of integrating our person, and in the sense of uniting with God. Thirdly, healing can be both metaphor and reality in Christian spirituality. As metaphor, it suggests that the Christian walk is the process of healing what is diseased or wounded, in the same sense that the man on the road to Jericho was cared for by the Samaritan and the inn keeper.[3] As reality, healing is an important experience for many whose prayers for physical or emotional healing bring noticeable results. Augustine's views and those of Pentacostalists use these images; Augustine uses them as metaphor, Pentacostalists as experience.

Travelling and returning are all involved in the metaphors of *walking*, *journeying*, *climbing* and *homing*. Living life through time has often been compared to moving through space, as in walking down a road. This is the image used by Paul when he speaks of walking in the Spirit. The journey underlies John Bunyan's classic allegory, *Pilgrim's Progress*. It suggests both that we are on the move, and have not arrived yet, and that we do have a destination. The image of climbing, whether a mountain or a ladder, is an ancient one, starting in Genesis, suggesting progress towards God, and being able to look back over one's path. This image does have problems, however, for those of us who see grace as the fundamental reality of the walk, from start to finish. It seems to imply an accomplishment which could be a temptation to pride in one's worthiness. Homing as an image does not focus on the travel, but on return and on settling into one's appropriate place. Some feminist writers have preferred this image, while the Roman Catholic medieval tradition has used a Neo-Platonic version of the journey: We came from God, and we are on our return journey to God.

Death and *resurrection* become metaphors for Christian falling away and restoration, sin and forgiveness, despair and hope. The death and resurrection of Jesus are seen as the type, or the powerful first instance of this pattern. Luther often spoke of daily baptism in these terms.[4] One might also consider the cycle of Israel's departure from God and return as fitting here.

We are told that a monk given thirty seconds to describe life in his monastery for a television interviewer replied, 'We fall down, then we get up. We fall down, then we get up. We fall down, then we get up. We fall down, then we get up...'

Battle has been a recurring image in discussions of Christian spirituality. The writer of Ephesians advises Christians to put on the whole armour of God to be able to stand against the wiles of the devil. Another view of the battle is Paul's internal struggle; different parts of himself are struggling in Romans 7. Later writers expanded on the theme of fighting with spiritual powers, with the 'old self', and with the powers of the world. Starting with Johann Arndt, Pietist and Evangelical writers have been accustomed to this image.

Finally, *thirst* and *hunger* suggest human need for the divine. Human beings are not self-sufficient, however much they may seek to be. It is God who is able to supply the 'bread of Life'[5] and 'water of life'.[6] Even the celebration demands wine at times![7]

These metaphors all help to give shape to our experiences, they give us a handle on interpreting our lives. Each needs the others; none is adequate by itself.

Questions about the global Christian community

One basic premise of this discussion is that Christianity is by nature a global rather than a European faith. We have looked at a few developments in selected continents to show that Christians can learn from one another across cultural, linguistic and racial lines.

But we must also say that even this glimpse of the variety of spiritualities leaves us with certain pressing questions. Among the first is the question of *unity in diversity*. Given that there are different styles of Christian living, can one speak of Christianity as a single religion? Isn't there a serious tension between the social activism of liberation theology and the quiet mysticism of Asian Christian mystics, who have used the methods of Hinduism or Buddhism?

A related question is how to evaluate different schools of spirituality from different cultures. Our basic stance in this book has been appreciation, welcoming the riches of different cultures to the Christian global family. But each of us in our own churches must make choices about the lifestyles we adopt. This also applies cross-culturally. What are the criteria for deciding if a given spirituality is authentically Christian, and if it is worthy to be emulated outside its own home? If North Americans have much to learn from Latin America, do Asians and Africans also have much to learn from each other?

Are the criteria for evaluating a spirituality the same or different from those for evaluating a theology? I would expect an authentic theology to reflect the Scriptures, to give a central role for Jesus as the Christ, to value faith, hope and love, to be understandable within its culture, and to challenge the idols of that culture. Are there additional criteria for spiritualities?

A third question is the way of *transmitting* spiritualities cross-culturally. Writing books can be helpful, but books seldom communicate beyond the specialist reader. Music, art and stories are effective ways of getting the spirit of another people. The exchange of living persons is perhaps the best means of sharing spiritualities. How can we more effectively share with one another what the Spirit has given us?

Finally, one of the fundamental issues for our future discussions will be if and how the Christian church can learn from *non-Christian movements and religions* to enhance its own spirituality. Has God given wisdom to other religious traditions? If so, how can Christians value and learn from them without diluting the integrity of their own tradition? I believe that there is much which has already been learned from other traditions in the past that we take for granted as Christians today. But there have also been cases in which adopting a spirituality from the outside has led to a distortion of the gospel, for example Neo-Platonism in European Christianity.

What is needed in our day?

Just as each period and culture in the history of Christian spirituality is unique, so we as individuals are different from one another. In our thirst for God, we need not all drink from the same kind of cup, glass, or goblet. A survey like this is intended to display the varieties of containers, but also to raise questions about their appropriateness for a given setting. Not all of them will be appropriate for Western nations on the verge of the twenty-first century.

A Christian spirituality for our time must keep the four relationships in balance. Neglecting creation can result in a disparagement of the self as well. Separating the creation relationship from the others, however, can lead to fanatical views about animal rights. Each of the four needs the others.

We also need a *listening spirituality*. We must be willing to hear the voices from continents and ages other than our own. It will be important that we also listen judiciously to peoples of other faiths. In North America this especially means listening to the native peoples of the continent and to people recovering from addictions. Without abandoning Christian commitments, it is possible to learn about spirituality that is ecologically healthy and holistically physical.

The focus of Christian spirituality must be *trinitarian*. A strong emphasis on the creator needs to supplement our clear, central devotion to Jesus Christ as incarnate redeemer, servant, healer and friend. The role of the Holy Spirit needs strong emphasis not only for the use of the spiritual gifts of many kinds, but also the sense of the presence of a powerful and loving God.

The basis of our spirituality in *God's passionate love* must be preserved against the constant tendency to make spirituality into a meritorious work. There is no doubt that we are called upon to respond to God's love. From the perspective of the onlooker, the behaviour of the Christian is what counts; spirituality is a behaviour, in so far as it involves praying, sharing one's goods, meditating, advocating the rights of the oppressed, going on retreats, receiving the sacraments, living simply, witnessing for the faith, reading the Bible, etc. Yet all of this is grounded not in our worthy intentions, but in God's forgiveness, God's empowerment, God's creation.

The Christian tradition has had serious blind spots. It is not that we in our day have none, but distance gives us a better perspective on those of other ages and cultures. One of those has been the acceptance of social norms about women that Jesus would not have approved. Another is the use of creation not as good stewards but exploiters. A third is the affirmation of a proper self-love which nourishes and has patience and forgiveness for oneself. Each of these blind spots were overcome in some part of the tradition, yet on the whole, the tradition still needs correcting here, in my view.

A personal word concludes the account

As I sit before my computer on a snowy Minnesota day surrounded by books, I am very much aware that this account of the tradition is only an introduction. It has been very good for me to do the reading which undergirds this telling of the story, but there is so much that I either want to read or ought to read. This distinction is because different parts of the tradition will be more helpful, more valid, more vivid, than others.

I have tried to give a balanced account of the Orthodox, Catholic and Protestant traditions. Including elements from all of them is important, I think, just as it is important to be aware of the whole Bible. Some parts which may not seem very useful at one time may be just what is needed at another. I think, for example, of the Lamentations and Lament Psalms, and how they fit with what contemporary psychologists have learned about our need to grieve. I think of the increasing role of Orthodox icons and the Jesus Prayer for Western Christians. I think of the spiritual power of African and Latin American Christianity for renewing Western Christians. Each of us needs the others, across time and space.

We have looked now at the story of Christian spirituality in many ages and lands. It has been an introduction to a world of study and prayer which invites us to drink deeper. Our thirst for God reflects a chronic dehydration. But God is longing to give us drink.

What then shall we do? Having a wider horizon for our practice of the Christian life, it is up to each of us to select, to experiment, to evaluate, to adapt. A kind of knowledge is available to us from books, but personal knowledge, the kind that really counts, can only come from experience. As my spiritual director likes to say, 'Spirituality is not something you study, but something you live!'

Recommended Reading

Paul Ofstedal, editor, *Daily Readings from Spiritual Classics*, Minneapolis: Augsburg, 1990.
Praying with... Hildegard of Bingen, Catherine of Sienna, Julian of Norwich, etc., Winona, Minnesota: St Mary's Press. (*Companions for the Journey* Series)

Appendix 1: Time Line

100	200	300	400	500	600	700	800	900	1000

Montanus
(c. 157)

Ignatius of Antioch
(160–220)

Tertullian
(160?–225)

Perpetua
(d. 200)

Alban
(d.c. 209 or 305)

Origen
(185–254)

Antony of Egypt
(250–353)

Athanasius
(296?–373)

Dionysius the Areopagite
(4th or 5th c.)

Ephrem
(306?–73)

Basil of Caesarea
(330–79)

Evagrius of Pontus
(345?–99)

Pelagius
(c.354–after 418)

Augustine
(354–430)

John Cassian
(360?–432)

Patrick
(389?–461?)

Brigid
(d.c. 523)

Benedict
(480–547)

Columba
(521–97)

Anselm of Canterbury
(1033–1109)

167

1100	1200	1300	1400	1500

Bernard of Clairvaux
(1090–1153)

Hildegard of Bingen
(1109–79)

Dominic Guzman
(1170?–1221)

Francis of Assisi
(1181/2–1226)

Clare of Assisi
(1193–1253)

Albert the Great
(c. 1200–80)

Bonaventure
(1217–74)

Thomas Aquinas
(1225–74)

Meister Eckhart
(1260?–1328?)

Jan Van Ruysbroeck
(1293–1381)

Gregory Palamas
(1296–1359)

Julian of Norwich
(1353–1416?)

Thomas à Kempis
(1380–1471)

Martin Luther
(1483–1546)

Ulrich Zwingli
(1484–1531)

Ignatius Loyola
(1491?–1556)

Menno Simons
(1496?–1561)

John Calvin
(1509–64)

Teresa of Avila
(1515–82)

John of the Cross
(1542–91)

Matteo Ricci
(1552–1610)

Johann Arndt
(1555–1621)

Lancelot Andrewes
(1555–1626)

Francis de Sales
(1567–1622)

John Donne
(1571–1631)

Pierre de Berulle
(1575–1629)

Roberto de Nobili
(1577–1656)

Johann Gerhard
(1582–1637)

George Herbert
(1593–1633)

APPENDIX 1: TIME LINE

| 1600 | 1700 | 1800 | 1900 | 2000 |

John Eudes
(1601–80)

Lawrence of the Resurrection
(1611–91)

Jeremy Taylor
(1613–67)

Blaise Pascal
(1623–62)

George Fox
(1624–91)

Miguel de Molinos
(b. 1628)

John Bunyan
(1628–88)

Philip Jacob Spener
(1635–1705)

Mme Jeanne Guyon
(1648–1717)

François Fenelon
(1651–1715)

August Herman Francke
(1663–1727)

John Wesley
(1703–91)

Charles Wesley
(1707–88)

John Woolman
(1720–72)

John Newton
(1725–1807)

Macarius of Corinth
(1731–1805)

**Nicodemus of the
Holy Mountain**
(1749–1809)

William Wilberforce
(1759–1833)

William Carey
(1761–1834)

John Keble
(1792–1866)

Henry Venn
(1796–1873)

Edward Pusey
(1800–82)

John Henry Newman
(1801–90)

Caroline Chisholm
(1808–77)

Søren Kierkegaard
(1813–55)

Kanzo Uchimura
(1861–1929)

William Wade Harris
(1865?–1929)

William Seymour
(1870–1922)

Evelyn Underhill
(1875–1941)

John Flynn
(1880–1951)

Paul Couterier
(1881–1953)

Toyohiko Kagawa
(1888–1960)

A.J. Appasamy
(1891–1975)

Alan Paton
(1903–88)

Dietrich Bonhoeffer
(1906–45)

Mother Teresa
(b. 1910)

Thomas Merton
(1915–68)

Bayers Naudé
(b. 1915)

Kazo Kitamori
(b. 1916)

Bukole Wa Ilunga
(b. 1920)

Martin Luther King
(1926–68)

Gustavo Gutierrez
(b. 1928)

Kosuke Koyama
(b. 1929)

Desmond Tutu
(b. 1931)

Matthew Fox
(b. 1940)

Appendix 2:
Spiritual Exercises

Chapter 1: Silence and Meditation

1. Determine to spend some time each day in quietness. Choose a place, either inside, for example in a favourite chair, or outside, where you can walk, jog, or ride a bike. Deliberately become aware of your body's rhythms, of breathing, heartbeat and muscle tension. Do not try to control your thoughts, but remain in a state of relaxed alertness. If you find your thoughts turning to upcoming activities, sexual fantasies, worries, or any other 'static', take the distraction as a sign of something coming to the surface, but return to your silence without being perturbed or blaming yourself.

As you do this exercise you will be able to calm and centre yourself more quickly and appreciate the silence for longer periods of time. This focusing in silence is a fundamental discipline of spiritualities, and provides the basis for others which require focusing, or paying attention. One may think of this silence as giving 'loving attention' to God and to oneself.

2. Meditation is focusing one's thoughts while at the same time being open to inspirations as they come. The object of meditation may be a natural phenomenon. For example one can sit by a lake, the sea, a meadow, or a forest and quietly observe and ponder. Or one can meditate on an event in one's own life or that of a biblical figure or saint. For Christians, meditating on Jesus and the events of his life is central. In the next chapter, the meditative reading of the Bible will be described as the exercise.

Aids for the Exercises

Richard J. Foster, *Celebration of Discipline: The Path to Spiritual Growth*, Hodder, 1989.

Richard J. Foster, *Challenge of the Disciplines*, San Francisco: Harper, 1989.

Richard J. Foster, *Prayers from the Heart*, Hodder, 1995.

These books contain sound advice about most of the exercises in these chapters. I highly recommend them.

Bradley Hanson, *The Call of Silence: Discovering Christian Meditation*, Minneapolis: Augsburg, 1980.

William E. Hulme, *Celebrating God's Presence: A Guide to Christian Meditation*, Minneapolis: Augsburg, 1988.
Ron and Lyn Klug, *Faithful Hearts, Faithful Hands*, Rejoice Curriculum for Adults, Minneapolis: Augsburg, 1992.

Chapter 2: Prayer, Reading and Pondering (Lectio Divina)

1. Take time for silence as in Chapter 1 to focus your attention and relax your body. Then deliberately raise your mind and heart to God. Become aware of God's presence, not somewhere above the ceiling, but indwelling you and all things. Spend some time without speaking to God, but just being in God's presence. (How do you feel about this?) Then speak as you will.

It may be helpful to follow the pattern of ACTS: Adoration, Confession, Thanksgiving, Supplication. Adoration means praise and vocal love expressed to God. Confession means naming the things that keep you from loving and trusting God, and receiving God's forgiveness. Thanksgiving may include the counting of all one's blessings. Supplication is asking for help, either for oneself or others.

There is no one right way to pray for all people, so do not get caught up in rigidly following the ACTS formula or any other. But it is important to attend to the various dimensions of prayer as indicated by these four letters, and perhaps others. Prayer gets to be very dry when it is only S's (Supplications).

If you do not pray much, it may be for a number of reasons. Perhaps a good spiritual counsellor can best help you diagnose the problems. One of them may be anger at God which goes unrecognized because of teachings that suggest it is wrong to be angry at God. Believe me, God is big enough to handle our anger! God still loves us even when we tell God how angry we feel. Just as with a human friend, such telling can clear the air and revitalize the relationship. My own tendency when I feel angry is not to admit the anger, but to withdraw from the person I am angry with, and be silent. This applies in the spiritual life when we withdraw from God and do not speak in prayer.

Prayer is communion with God, and deserves a lifetime of learning. Do not let guilty feelings over past neglect prevent you from trying it anew.

2. *Lectio divina* is the practice of reading aloud in a slow and meditative way. Benedict's monastic Rule emphasizes its importance. Choose a short

passage of Scripture which stands out for you. Read aloud a psalm or a chapter from one of the Gospels of the New Testament. Stop when you come to a verse which seems especially meaningful. Then turn it over in your mind, seeking the ways in which it might encourage, convict, or liberate you. Use your imagination. Picture yourself with God or with other characters in the story. Picture your own situation with a human character, Jesus, acting in it. Then listen and observe what happens.

Aids for the Exercises

Anthony Bloom, *Beginning to Pray*, New York: Paulist Press, 1970.
Bradley Hanson, *Teach Us to Pray: Overcoming Obstacles to Daily Prayer*, Minneapolis: Augsburg, 1990.
Thomas Merton, *Praying the Psalms*, Collegeville, Minnesota: The Liturgical Press, 1986.

Chapter 3: Communal Worship and Fasting

1. 'Going to church' may be very significant for your personal spirituality or it may be irrelevant, depending on what you make of it. The Christian walk is not ideally a private walk; it means being part of a people, an organic 'body of Christ' which extends down through the centuries and over all continents. The local community of faith which you choose is an expression of that 'body'. It should be a place where you are known, accepted, loved, challenged, made accountable. The worship experiences which you share will be focused on word and sacrament. Hearing the law and gospel preached is important for one's growth, as well as receiving the Lord's Supper (sometimes called the Eucharist, Holy Communion, or Mass).

Be intentional about your church attendance. Do not simply go through the motions. If you are attending a church which does not provide a meaningful worship experience, then try to change things. Or perhaps a different congregation or even denomination can better meet your need. One cannot simply sit back and expect a congregation to serve the individual; churches are places to give service, not simply to be 'spiritually entertained'. But it is a good idea to visit a number of different church traditions to see the variety of ways in which God is worshipped. A balance of intellect and emotion is needed, according to different tastes.

Before attending a church service, take time to meditate about your intentions. Seek the presence of God and a genuine meeting with the people. Have a prayerful attitude during the service, with an open ear. When you sing a hymn, really praise God through it. On some occasions that praise will be more precious than any other part of the service. On other days the bread and wine of the Eucharist will be most meaningful. The preacher may speak just the word you need on other occasions. But it is not often that all of these things will happen in one service. So it takes a kind of patience to be in a Christian worshipping community. Some days our hearts are cold, the sermon is boring, and no one makes contact with us. On other days the music and the Spirit invade our hearts.

2. An ascetic practice usually goes against the grain. It exercises the power to say No to a familiar practice. Care must be taken to recognize the goodness of something which one will do without for a limited period of time.

One of the oldest types of self-denial is fasting. I recommend that any healthy person can find value in fasting, but it should be done with good guidance, and moderately to start. It is very important to take in enough fluids. (Remember the first paragraph of this book!) Fasting may not prove immediately helpful. Try it a few times to see the pattern that best fits you. Partial fasts may be more helpful than complete fasts. Fasting is not a good way to try to lose weight, but when done properly, it can indeed bring into focus the real values of life. There is a sense of interdependence with others and dependence on God which can result. It is also wise to use the time normally devoted to eating to the practice of another spiritual discipline, such as prayer or reading. Fasting can increase one's sense of freedom and strength. One discovers, 'I can *choose* to eat or not to eat.'

Aids for the Exercises

James Lee Beall, *The Adventure of Fasting: A Practical Guide*, Old Tappan, New Jersey: Revel, 1974.

Richard J. Foster, 'Fasting', 'Confession', 'Worship', 'Guidance' and 'Celebration' in *Celebration of Discipline*, revised edition, San Francisco: Harper, 1988, pages 47–61, 125–71.

Patrick R. Kiefert, *Welcoming the Stranger: A Public Theology of Worship and Evangelism* Minneapolis: Fortress, 1992.

Chapter 4: The 'Jesus Prayer' and Icons

1. Quiet yourself as in the first exercise. Start by giving voice to the prayer by repeating 'Lord Jesus, have mercy on me.' You may wish to think the words silently, using the first phrase while inhaling and the second phrase while

exhaling. Be careful to adapt the prayer to your normal breathing, rather than trying to keep up your breathing to the rate of the prayer. You may find yourself hyperventilating if this happens. Although the words suggest contrition, the prayer may be used in any mood, whether of joy and thanksgiving or sorrow and grief. Try praying this prayer for twenty minutes each morning and evening.

2. Icons provide a 'right brain' approach to prayer. They give an image instead of words. Select an icon. First spend time centring yourself in silence, then put yourself in the presence of the icon. Regard it not as a simple picture but as a window through which you are steadily communing with another person. Put yourself on the other side of the window, and look at yourself lovingly, with all your faults and difficulties. Contemplate the other and yourself with compassion.

Aids for the Exercises

John Baggley, *Doors of Perception: Icons and their Spiritual Significance*, Crestwood, New York: St Vladimir's Seminary Press, 1988.
Simon Barrington-Ward, *The Jesus Prayer*, Bible Reading Fellowship, 1996.
Henri J.M. Nouwen, *Behold the Beauty of the Lord: Praying with Icons*, Notre Dame, Indiana: Ave Maria Press, 1987.
Lev Gillet, *The Jesus Prayer*, Crestwood, New York: St Vladimir's Seminary Press, 1987.
Per Olof Sjogren, *The Jesus Prayer*, SPCK, 1975.

Chapter 5: The Lord's Prayer and the Examen

From Luther we learn of his simple method of prayer, and from Ignatius, the concept of the daily examen.

1. Spend some time in silence as discussed in Exercise 1. Now take the Lord's Prayer one phrase at a time, and 'make a garland' for each one as Luther suggested. For each phrase, think of something to give thanks for, something to repent of, and some guidance for daily life. Then go on to the next phrase. If one thought is especially precious, stay with it. Don't worry about finishing the whole prayer.

2. The daily examen may be done in a variety of ways, but here is one which is helpful to me. At bedtime, briefly review the day, looking especially for 'grace notes' from God and for problems which have arisen. Then the next morning examine the previous day in more detail. Use these words to guide your thinking: Insight, Review, Thanks, Repentance and Renewal. First ask

God the Holy Spirit for insight, for we do not really know ourselves very well. Seek to recognize what your own inclinations might pass over, whether gifts, strengths, or sins. Then review the events of the day. Give thinks for all the gifts of the day. Repent and ask forgiveness for wrong choices or bad attitudes; ask for healing of neurotic guilt or broken relationships. Renewal means receiving God's forgiveness and strength for a new day as well as making very practical resolutions about what will help you in this day to avoid the pitfalls you have experienced before.

It is very helpful to write down briefly some points each day which arise from the examen.

Aids for the Exercises

Martin Luther, 'A Simple Way to Pray', *Luther's Works*, Philadelphia: Fortress, 1968, volume 43, pages 187–212.
Walter Trobisch, 'Martin Luther's Quiet Time', *Complete Works of Walter Trobisch*, Downers Grove, Illinois: Intervarsity, 1987, pages 703–14.

Chapter 6: Journalling and Spiritual Direction

1. Seventeenth and eighteenth-century Christians were faithful in their journalling. They recorded not only the outer events of their lives, but also their inner thoughts and feelings.

Putting things on paper is one way to get them out where they can be dealt with. It is especially helpful to write out prayers. Experiment by writing the longings of your heart in a prayer to God. It takes longer than speaking, of course, but this gives you time to ponder.

2. A spiritual mentor can be a very important help in the spiritual journey. The guilt and shame which we seek to hide can be accepted, discussed, healed in a situation of trust and openness. The gifts and possibilities we are not aware of can be pointed out. Encouragement when life is tough can be very important. Most of all, the grace of God, which we seem to forget again and again, flows through.

The 'soul friend' or 'spiritual director' can be a specially trained counsellor, or more informally a respected friend. Some spiritual directors see their clients about every three weeks. Some receive a fee for their work, while others do not. Serving as a companion to another wayfarer is holy work, and especially gratifying when the discernment of God's gracious leading bears fruit.

Aids for the Exercises

Christina Baldwin, *One to One: Self-Understanding through Journal Writing*, M. Evans, 1991.

Tilden Edwards, *Spiritual Friend*, New York: Paulist Press, 1980.

Ronald Klug, *How to Keep a Spiritual Journal*, Nashville, Thomas Nelson, 1982.

Kenneth Leech, *Soul Friend: The Practice of Christian Spirituality*, San Francisco: Harper, 1980.

Edward C. Sellner, *Mentoring: The Ministry of Spiritual Kinship*, Notre Dame, Indiana: Ave Maria Press, 1990.

Chapter 7: Simple Living and Writing a Letter

1. Living simply means consuming less in order to share more. It means not rushing to jam as much activity into each hour as possible. It means not wasting energy or food or possessions, so as to live in better harmony with the earth. For most Westerners following such a simple life style would involve fundamental changes in daily life. Doing so is a matter of a process, not an absolute.

Begin by identifying one aspect of your life that could be 'simplified'. Sometimes it is in fact more complicated to recycle than to throw away, to repair than to replace, to bicycle rather than drive. Finding ways to cut your own and your household's consumption and waste is nevertheless a worthwhile project. Start with only one part of your lifestyle, before taking on the whole.

How you spend your money is a very important part of your spirituality. Giving away a significant fraction of your income to spiritual communities and to those in need is a practical sign of your spiritual commitment.

'Spending' time is also a sign of what you value most. Think through the times you have spun your wheels by rushing about, and see if there is a way to go at life more calmly. Taking time for the sky, the grass, and people who are important to you is part of a simple lifestyle.

2. In our day when citizens of democratic states have influence on national policies, writing letters can be an important spiritual exercise. Advocating the rights of those who have been denied is being a kind of preventive 'good Samaritan'. For example, Bread for the World advocates for the hungry both in the USA and globally. Amnesty International advocates for prisoners of conscience who are often tortured or 'disappeared'. The Children's Defense Fund stands for the rights of the young. Writing letters is an effective way to stand up for justice and love in our world of poverty, refugees, and prisoners.

Aids for the Exercises

Amy Dacyczyn, *Tightwad Gazette*, New York: Villard, 1993.

John W. De Gruchy, editor, *Cry Justice!: Prayers, Meditations and Readings from South Africa*, Maryknoll, NY: Orbis, 1988.

Duane Elgin, *Voluntary Simplicity: Toward a Way of Life that is Outwardly Simple, Inwardly Rich*, New York: Wm Morrow, 1981.

Delores Histand Friesen, *Living More with Less: Study/Action Guide*, Scottdale, Pennsylvania: Herald Press, 1981.

Doris Janzen Longacre, *Living More with Less*, Scottdale, Pennsylvania: Herald Press, 1980.

Mary Schramm, 'A Wonderful Word: Enough', *Extravagant Love*, Minneapolis: Augsburg, 1988, pages 74–85.

Chapter 8: Service and Vocation

On the basis of your love for other people, volunteer your time to help those in need. There is a vast array of opportunities for Westerners here. One may help a shelter for battered women, staff a centre that gives food, clothing or shelter to the homeless, tutor students with their school lessons or in learning English. This interaction with other people is an important spiritual exercise which feeds into the life of prayer.

You are called by God to trust God's love, to act with love for others. You have a calling as a parent or child. You may also be called to a particular occupation, in order to reflect these prior calls. Working in the world whether in the home, office, school, or factory is a vocation from God. Spirituality involves the way one views one's work to express the core of one's values. Consider how your work experience with all of its difficulties can be the place where creative accomplishment and compassion give glory to God.

Aids for the Exercises

William E. Diehl, *The Monday Connection: A Spirituality of Competence, Affirmation, and Support in the Workplace*, San Francisco: Harper, 1991.

Donald Heiges, *The Christian's Calling*, second edition, Philadelphia: Fortress, 1984.

Lee Hordy, *The Fabric of this World*, Grand Rapids, Michigan: Eerdmans, 1990.

Glossary

anamchara A Celtic word for 'soul friend', a spiritual companion and guide.

anchorite, anchoress A man or woman who chooses to live alone to pray and meditate.

Anglican Relating to the Church of England.

apatheia Literally 'passionlessness'. In practice, freedom from passions which drive one away from God.

apophatic An approach to spirituality which emphasizes the mystery of God, and therefore 'strips away' all words and metaphors for God in order to meet God in silence and darkness.

canon The accepted collection of Christian writings—'the canon of Scripture'.

cenobitic Communal monasticism as opposed to individual; opposite of eremitic.

Chalcedon A church council in 451 which defined Jesus Christ as one Person with two natures—one human, one divine.

charism, charismatic A charism is a gracious gift from God, such as those discussed by Paul in 1 Corinthians 12. Charismatic Christians value and employ these gifts. Charismatic may more specifically refer to those people in historic denominations who employ these gifts, as distinct from Pentecostalists who have founded denominations which employ them. In a wider sense, every Christian is charismatic, having received such gifts.

contextualize To develop a form of Christianity which is culturally fitting.

Diaspora, the The dispersion of the Jews to other nations primarily between the 8th and 6th centuries BC.

docetic Refers to the idea that Jesus only appeared to be human; affirms that spirit must not come into contact with body; one aspect of Gnosticism.

Eastern Orthodox Those churches such as Greek Orthodox or Russian Orthodox which accept the first seven ecumenical councils as valid, including the definition of Chalcedon. (Roman Catholics accept more councils than seven.)

Ecumenical 1. Referring to the whole inhabited world, universal. 2. The movement to unite different denominations.

eremitic The form of monasticism in which persons live alone. The word hermit comes from this word.

eschatology The study of the destiny of humanity and the creation, the consummation of all things.

Gnosticism A variety of religious movements judged to be heretical by the early church which denied the goodness of the world and taught a secret knowledge for escaping from the world at death.

Hellenism A general word for the Greek culture spread widely by Alexander the Great in the fourth century BC.

icon A painting of a religious figure which serves as a point of contact with the worshipper; an object of devotion but not worship which affirms the incarnation of Christ.

incarnation The teaching that the Word of God became flesh in Jesus of Nazareth; a strong affirmation of the goodness of human, physical life. Not to be confused with reincarnation in Hinduism.

Jansenism A religious movement in France which taught the predestination of the saved and the unsaved.

justification Being made right with God; or, the declaration that one is righteous on the basis of Christ's death and resurrection; a gift to be received by faith.

kataphatic An approach to spirituality which makes full use of words and images to describe God.

liberation theology A movement which sees the goal of the gospel as human freedom from spiritual, political and economic oppression. May be applied by any oppressed group, e.g. Women's Liberation, Gay Liberation, etc.

martyr A witness to the faith who is put to death.

mendicant Begging; a characteristic of early Franciscan and Dominican orders in their desire to embrace a life of voluntary poverty.

monasticism A movement to seek Christian perfection by leaving one's society and devoting oneself to worship, prayer and good works.

Montanism Following Montanus, a movement which had very strict ascetical standards, the expectation of the imminent return of Christ, and the practice of charismatic phenomena, especially prophecy.

mysticism A type of spirituality which seeks union with God or the Ultimate. As commonly used, it may include any supernatural phenomena such as visions and voices, but Christian mystics warned against focusing attention on these.

Neo-Platonism A later form of Plato's teaching developed by Plotinus and others, with a more mystical and religious emphasis than Plato's original philosophy.

Nicea The Council of Nicea in 325 was the first Ecumenical Council, called by Emperor Constantine to settle doctrinal disputes among divided Christians. Among other things, the council agreed to a statement that the Son was of the same Being as the Father. This later became the basis for the statement we know as the Nicene Creed, a fundamental development in the doctrine of the Trinity.

Oriental Orthodox Churches in Asia and Africa which did not accept the definitions of Chalcedon and came to be separated from the Eastern Orthodox churches.

pantheism The view that all things are God and God is all things. The distinction between creator and creation is eliminated.

panentheism The view that God is in all things and all things are in God.

parousia The second coming of Christ.

Philokalia 'The love of beauty'; title of collections of Eastern spiritual writings first by Basil in the fourth century, and later by others in the eighteenth century.

paradox A striking truth which may be expressed in seemingly contradictory statements.

Pelagianism Following Pelagius, a view that people are capable and responsible for working out their own salvation, instead of needing to rely solely on God's grace for salvation. This view was opposed by Augustine and later by the Protestant churches.

Pietism A renewal movement in seventeenth-century Lutheran and Reformed churches which emphasized Bible study, conversion, prayer meetings in homes, institutions to help the needy, friendship across denominational lines, and world mission. The movement later was seen as legalistic, separatist, and sentimental; the word is commonly used to refer to this later type of spirituality.

Quietism A movement in seventeenth-century Roman Catholicism which was condemned for its alleged indifference to all things, including personal salvation.

rosary A set of beads with a small crucifix used as a devotional aid by Roman Catholics and others, to pray the Hail Mary and Our Father prayers while meditating on the events of Mary's and Jesus' lives.

Trent A council of the Roman Catholic Church which responded to the Protestant Reformation. It was held in Trent, northern Italy from 1548 to 1563.

Western Church The church of the western Mediterranean, specifically the Roman Catholic Church, and later the Protestant churches which separated from it.

Vatican II The Second Vatican Council, held in Rome at the Vatican from 1962 to 1965.

Endnotes

Chapter 1
Spirituality and Christianity
(page 11)

1. John, chapter 4.

2. John 7:37–39.

3. Henry Nouwen, 'Foreword' to Gustavo Gutierrez, *We Drink from Our Own Wells*, Maryknoll, New York: Orbis, pages xx, xxi.

4. Philip Sheldrake, *Spirituality and History: Questions of Interpretation and Method*, New York: Crossroad, 1992.

5. Gordon Wakefield, *Westminster Dictionary of Christian Spirituality*, Philadelphia: Westminster, 1983, page v.

6. Wakefield, *Westminster Dictionary*, pages 361–62.

7. Galatians 5:25 (RSV).

8. Jaroslav Pelikan, *The Vindication of Tradition*, New Haven: Yale, 1984, page 65.

9. C.S. Lewis, 'Introduction' in *The Incarnation of the Word of God: Being the Treatise of St Athanasius' De Incarnatione Verbi Dei*, New York: Macmillan, 1947, pages 6–7.

Chapter 2
Four Relationships in the Bible
(page 28)

1. See Mark 12:28–31; Deuteronomy 6:4–5.

2. Exodus 33:11, 20 (NRSV).

3. Isaiah 40:28–29 (NRSV).

4. Isaiah 55:9 (NRSV).

5. Genesis 1–2 and many other places.

6. Exodus 1–15.

7. Psalm 96.

8. Psalm 27.

9. Isaiah 6.

10. Romans 8:38 (RSV).

11. Romans 11:33, 36 (RSV).

12. Genesis 1:1—2:4a and 2:4b–25.

13. 1 John 2:16 (RSV).

14. Romans 8:19–25.

Chapter 3
The Beginnings of a Global
Community (page 36)

1. Acts 1:8 (NRSV).

2. Acts 10:44–48a (NRSV).

3. 1 Corinthians 9:24–25 (NRSV).

4. James Hamilton Charlesworth, editor, *The Old Testament Pseudepigrapha*, Garden City, New York: Doubleday, 1985, volume 2, pages 726–27.

5. Charlesworth, *The Old Testament Pseudepigrapha*, page 749.

6. Charlesworth, *The Old Testament Pseudepigrapha*, pages 752–53.

7. 1 Corinthians 12:7–11.

8. Matthew 6:1–4, 16–18.

9. Matthew 5:27–30.

10. Matthew 16:24.

11. 1 Corinthians 7:2–3

12. Tertullian, *Disciplinary, Moral and Ascetical Works*, New York: Fathers of the Church, Inc., 1959, page 103.

13. Sebastian Brock, 'Introduction' in Saint Ephrem's *Hymns on Paradise*, Crestwood, New York: St Vladimir's Seminary Press, 1990, pages 25–32.

14. Brock, 'Introduction', page 40.

15. Brock, 'Introduction', page 48.

16. 2 Peter 1:4 (NRSV).

17. Brock, 'Introduction', page 73. Quotation from Hymns on Virginity (XLVIII. 17–18).

18. See, for example, Benedicta Ward's translation, *The Desert Christian: Sayings of the Desert Fathers: The Alphabetical Collection*, New York: Macmillan, 1980; or Thomas Merton's selection, *The Wisdom of the Desert: Sayings from the Desert Fathers of the Fourth Century*, Norfolk, Connecticut: New Directions, 1960. Also see Helen Waddell's *The Desert Fathers*, New York: Sheed and Ward, 1942).

19. Benedicta Ward, translator, *The Desert Christian: Sayings of the Desert Fathers: The*

Alphabetical Collection, New York: Macmillan, 1980, page 72.

20. Ward, *The Desert Christian*, page 193.

21. Ward, *The Desert Christian*, page 194.

22. Ward, *The Desert Christian*, page 196.

23. Gregory of Nyssa, 'Life of St Macrina', in *Ascetical Works*, Washington, DC: Catholic University of America Press, 1966, *Fathers of the Church*, volume 58, pages 163–91.

24. Kallistos Ware, 'Ways of Prayer and Contemplation: I. Eastern' in McGinn, Meyendorff and Leclercq, editors, *Christian Spirituality: Origins to the Twelfth Century*, New York: Crossroad, 1987, page 398.

25. Ludwig Bieler, translator, *The Works of St Patrick*, (Ancient Christian Writers), volume 17, 1953), pages 70–71.

26. Edward C. Sellner, *Mentoring: The Ministry of Spiritual Kinship*, Notre Dame, Indiana: Ave Maria Press, 1990, pages 61–75.

27. James 5:16 (NRSV).

28. Esther de Waal, editor, *The Celtic Vision: Prayers and Blessings from the Outer Hebrides*, Darton, Longman & Todd, 1988, page 145.

29. Pseudo-Dionysius, 'The Divine Names', in *Pseudo-Dionysius: The Complete Works*, New York: Paulist Press, 1987, pages 49–50.

30. 'The Mystical Theology' in *Pseudo-Dionysius: The Complete Works*, page 135.

Chapter 4
The European Era (page 71)

1. Luke 18:13 (NRSV).

2. 1 Thessalonians 5:17 (NRSV).

3. Acts 4:10, 12 (NRSV).

4. Kallistos Ware, 'The Origins of the Jesus Prayer: Diadochus, Gaza, Sinai' in *The Study of Spirituality*, edited by Cheslyn Jones, Geoffrey Wainwright and Edward Yarnold, New York: Oxford University Press, 1986, page 176.

5. Ware, 'The Origins of the Jesus Prayer', page 184.

6. *Nicene and Post-Nicene Fathers*, Grand Rapids, Michigan: Eerdmans, 1959, volume 14, page 549.

7. Athanasius, 'On the Incarnation of the Word' in *The Christology of the Later Fathers*,

edited by E.R. Hardy, Philadelphia: Westminster, 1954, pages 55–110.

8. Anselm, *Proslogion*, chapter 2

9. Thomas Merton, *The Last of the Fathers: Saint Bernard of Clairvaux and the Encyclical Letter, Doctor Mellifluus*, New York: Harcourt, Brace and Co., 1954, page 93.

10. Bernard of Clairvaux, *On Loving God*, chapters 8–11.

11. Bernard of Clairvaux, *Sermons on the Song of Songs*, Sermon LXIX, SCM Press, 1959, pages 117–18.

12. Ingrid H. Shafer, *Eros and the Womanliness of God: Andrew Greeley's Romances of Renewal*, Chicago: Loyola University Press, 1986.

13. Bernard of Clairvaux, *Sermons on the Song of Songs*, 108–9.

14. Thomas à Kempis, *The Imitation of Christ*, Baltimore: Penguin Books, 1975, 3:37.

15. Matthew Fox, OP, *Breakthrough: Meister Eckhart's Creation Spirituality in New Translation*, Garden City, New York: Image Books, 1980, page 39.

16. Jan van Ruysbroeck, *Spiritual Espousals*, I: xxxvi, Faber and Faber, 1952, page 82.

17. Jan van Ruysbroeck, *Sparkling Stone*, VIII

18. Ruysbroeck, *Sparkling Stone*, XIII

19. Ruysbroeck, *Spiritual Espousals*, II: viii.

20. Julian of Norwich, *Showings*, New York: Paulist Press, 1978, Long Text, pages 52–63.

21. Julian of Norwich, *Showings*, page 342.

Chapter 5
Protestant and Catholic Reform (page 89)

1. Bengt R. Hoffman, *Luther and the Mystics: A Re-examination of Luther's Spiritual Experience and his Relation to the Mystics*, Minneapolis: Augsburg, 1976.

2. Martin Luther, 'The Freedom of a Christian' in *Martin Luther's Basic Theological Writings*, edited by Timothy F. Lull, Minneapolis: Fortress, 1989, page 596.

3. Walter Trobisch, 'Martin Luther's Quite Time', in *Complete Works of Walter Trobisch*, Downers Grove, Illinois: Intervarsity, 1987, pages 703–14.

4. Sermon on Job, *Opera Calvini* 34, column

316; Commentary on Isaiah 42:14, *Opera Calvini* 36, column 69.

5. Paul V. Marshall, 'The Anglican Tradition' in *Protestant Spiritual Traditions*, edited by Frank C. Senn, New York: Paulist, 1986, page 133.

6. *The Collected Works of St John of the Cross*, translated by Kieran Kavanaugh and Otilio Rodriguez, Washington, DC:ICS Publications, Institute of Carmelite Studies, 1979, pages 711–12.

Chapter 6
The 'Modern' Era (page105)

1. Darrell Jodock, *The Church's Bible: Its Contemporary Authority*, Minneapolis: Fortress, 1989, pages 16–19.

2. John Wesley, *The Journals of John Wesley: A Selection*, edited by Elisabeth Jay, New York: Oxford University Press, 1987, pages 34–35.

3. See for example Matthew 5:48 and 1 John 3:4–10.

4. Brother Lawrence of the Resurrection, *The Practice of the Presence of God*, Westminster, Maryland: Newman Press, 1952, page 107.

5. Thomas Merton, 'Reflections on the Character and Genius of Fenelon', in *Fenelon's Letters of Love and Counsel*, New York: Harcourt Brace, and World, 1964, pages 9–30.

6. Fenelon, *Letters of Love and Counsel*, pages 216–18.

7. Fenelon, *Letters of Love and Counsel*, page 289.

8. *Pensées* 423.

9. *The Way of a Pilgrim: And the Pilgrim Continues His Way*, translated by R.M. French, New York: Harper, 1952?, pages 6–9.

Chapter 7
The Twentieth Century (page 123)

1. See Luke 3:16; Acts 1:5.

2. William A. Dyrness, *Learning about Theology from the Third World*, Grand Rapids, Michigan: Zondervan, 1990.

3. Susan Rakoczy, IHM, *Common Journey, Different Paths: Spiritual Direction in Cross-Cultural Perspective*, Maryknoll, New York: Orbis, 1992.

4. Vincent J. Donovan, *Christianity Rediscovered: An Epistle from the Masai*, Notre Dame, Indiana: Fides/Claretian, 1978.

5. Jon Sobrino, *Spirituality of Liberation: Toward Political Holiness*, Maryknoll, New York: Orbis, 1988.

6. Bukole Wa Ilunga, *Paths of Liberation: A Third World Spirituality*, Maryknoll, New York: Orbis, 1985, page 36.

7. Charles Villa-Vicentio, *Trapped in Apartheid*, Grand Rapids, Michigan: Eerdmans, 1989.

8. John de Gruchy, editor, *Cry Justice!: Prayers, Meditations and Readings from South Africa*, Maryknoll, New York: Orbis, 1986.

9. de Gruchy, *Cry Justice!*, pages 64–66.

10. Desmond Tutu, editor, *An African Prayer Book*, New York/London: Doubleday, 1995, pages 65–66, 80, 87–92.

11. Tutu, *An African Prayer Book*, page 134.

12. Zephaniah Kameeta, *Why, O Lord?: Psalms and Sermons from Namibia*, Philadelphia: Fortress, 1986, page 30.

13. Gordon Mackay Haliburton, *The Prophet Harris: A Study of an African Prophet and his Mass-movement in the Ivory Coast and the Gold Coast 1913–1915*, New York: Oxford University Press, 1973.

14. Kosuke Koyama, *Waterbuffalo Theology*, Maryknoll, New York: Orbis, 1974.

15. Kosuke Koyama, *Three Mile an Hour God*, Maryknoll, New York: Orbis, 1979.

16. Kosuke Koyama, *Mount Fuji and Mount Sinai: A Critique of Idols*, Maryknoll, New York: Orbis, 1984.

17. Kazoh Kitamori, *Theology of the Pain of God*, Richmond, Virginia: John Knox Press, 1958, page 79.

18. Norimichi Ebizawa, editor, *Japanese Witnesses for Christ*, World Christian Books, New York: Association Press, 1957, page 56.

19. Ebizawa, *Japanese Witnesses for Christ*, page 61.

20. Jesse M. Trout, *Kagawa, Japanese Prophet*, World Christian Books, New York:

Association Press, 1959, page 25, quoted from *Song of the Slums*, SCM Press, 1935, pages 21f.

21. Trout, *Kagawa, Japanese Prophet*, page 63, quoted from *Brotherhood Economics*, SCM Press, 1937, page 108.

22. Trout, *Kagawa, Japanese Prophet*, page 28, quoted from *Love, the Law of Life*, SCM Press, 1930, pages 311–13.

23. G. Thompson Brown, *Christianity in the People's Republic of China*, Atlanta: John Knox, 1983, page 200.

24. Matthew 25.

25. G.W. Tromph, editor, *The Gospel is not Western: Black Theologies from the Southwest Pacific*, Maryknoll, New York: Orbis, 1987, page 94.

26. Muriel Porter, *Land of the Spirit? The Australian Religious Experience*, Geneva: Risk Book series, WCC Publications, 1990, page 93.

27. Tromph, *The Gospel is not Western*, page 40.

28. Galatians 3:28 (RSV).

29. Dennis C. Morreim, *Changed Lives: The Story of Alcoholics Anonymous*, Minneapolis: Augsburg, 1992.

30. Ernest Kurtz, *Not-God: A History of Alcoholics Anonymous*, Center City, Minnesota: Hazeldon, 1979.

31. *Alcoholics Anonymous*, third edition, New York: AA World Services, pages 59–60.

32. Dennis C. Morreim, *The Road to Recovery: Bridges Between the Bible and the Twelve Steps*, Minneapolis: Augsburg, 1990.

33. Matthew 5.

34. Reinhold Niebuhr, 'Written for a service in the Congregational Church of Heath, Massachusetts, where Dr Niebuhr spent many summers, the prayer was first published in a monthly bulletin of the Federal Council of Churches', John Bartlett, *Familiar Quotations*, fifteenth edition, Boston: Little, Brown, 1980, page 823.

35. Gerald May, *Addiction and Grace*, San Francisco: Harper, 1988.

36. Romans 7:19 (JB).

37. Matthew Fox, OP, *Breakthrough: Meister Eckhart's Creation Spirituality in New Translation*, Garden City, New York: Image Books, 1980, pages 43–48.

38. Fox, *Breakthrough*, page 4.

39. Matthew Fox, 'Creation Centered Spirituality', in *Westminster Dictionary of Christian Spirituality*, Philadelphia: Westminster, 1983, page 100.

Chapter 8
Where Do We Go from Here?
(page 159)

1. Allan H. Sager, *Gospel-Centered Spirituality: An Introduction to Our Spiritual Journey*, Minneapolis: Augsburg, 1990, page 36.

2. Cheslyn Jones, Geoffrey Wainwright and Edward Yarnold, editors, *The Study of Spirituality*, New York: Oxford University Press, 1986, pages 592–605.

3. Luke 10:25–37.

4. See Romans 6:1–11.

5. John 6.

6. John 7.

7. John 3.

Select Bibliography

Allchin, A.M., *The Kingdom of Love and Knowledge: The Encounter Between Orthodoxy and the West*, New York: Seabury, 1982.

Appasamy, A.J., *Christianity as Bhakti Marga: A Study in the Mysticism of the Johannine Writings*, Macmillan, 1927.

Appasamy, A.J., *The Gospel and India's Heritage*, SPCK, 1942.

Bernard of Clairvaux, *On Loving God: And Selections from Sermons*, SCM Press, 1959.

Bieler, Ludwig, translator, *The Works of St Patrick*, Ancient Christian Writers, 1953, volume 17, pages 70–71.

Bosch, David J., *Transforming Mission: Paradigm Shifts in Theology of Mission*, Maryknoll, New York: Orbis, 1991.

Bouyer, Louis, *The Spirituality of the New Testament and the Fathers*, New York: Desclee, 1963. (Volume 1 of *A History of Christian Spirituality*)

Bouyer, Louis, *Orthodox Spirituality and Protestant and Anglican Spirituality*, New York: Desclee, 1969. (Volume 3 of *A History of Christian Spirituality*)

Boyd, R.H.S., *An Introduction to Indian Christian Theology*, Madras, Christian Literature Society, 1969.

Brock, Sebastian, translator, *The Syriac Fathers on Prayer and the Spiritual Life*, Kalamazoo, Michigan: Cistercian, 1987.

Brooks, Peter, editor, *Christian Spirituality: Essays in Honour of Gordon Rupp*, SCM Press, 1975.

Bynum, Caroline Walker, *Jesus as Mother: Studies in the Spirituality of the High Middle Ages*, Berkeley, California: University of California, 1982.

Charlesworth, James Hamilton, editor, *The Old Testament Pseudepigrapha*, Darton, Longman and Todd, 1990.

Charlesworth, James Hamilton, editor and translator, *The Odes of Solomon: The Syriac Texts*, Missoula, Montana: Scholars Press,

1977, pages 70–71. (Society of Biblical Literature, Texts and Translations 13, Pseudepigrapha Series 7)

Christensen, Bernhard, *The Inner Pilgrimage*, Minneapolis: Augsburg, 1975.

Dacyczyn, Amy, *Tightwad Gazette*, New York: Villard, 1993.

De Sales, Francis, *Introduction to the Devout Life*.

Donovan, Vincent J., *Christianity Rediscovered: An Epistle from the Masai*, SCM Press, 1992.

Dupre, Louis and Don E. Saliers, editors, *Christian Spirituality: Post Reformation and Modern*, New York: Crossroad, 1989. (Volume 18 of *World Spirituality*)

Dupre, Louis and James A. Wiseman, editors, *Light from Light: An Anthology of Christian Mysticism*, Paulist Press, 1993.

Elder, E. Rozanne, editor, *The Spirituality of Western Christendom*, Kalamazoo, Michigan: Cistercian, 1976.

Elgin, Duane, *Voluntary Simplicity: Toward a Way of Life that is Outworldly Simple, Inwardly Rich*, New York, Wm Morrow, 1981.

Erb, Peter C., editor, *Pietists: Selected Writings*, New York: Paulist, 1983. (*Classics of Western Spirituality* Series)

Ferguson, Duncan, editor, *New Age Spirituality: An Assessment*, Louisville, Kentucky: Westminster/John Knox, 1993.

Fremantle, Anne, editor, *The Protestant Mystics*, New York: New American Library, 1964.

French, R.M., translator, *The Way of a Pilgrim: And the Pilgrim Continues His Way*, New York: Harper, 1952(?).

Friesen, Delores Histand, *Living More with Less: Study/Action Guide*, Scottdale, PA: Herald Press, 1981.

Gannon, Thomas M. and George W. Traub, *The Desert and the City: An Interpretation of the History of Christian Spirituality*, New York: Macmillan, 1969.

Gonzonlez, Justo L., *A History of Christian Thought*, 3 volumes, New York: Abingdon, 1970–75.

Graef, Hilda, *The Light and the Rainbow: A Study in Christian Spirituality from its Roots in the Old Testament and its Development through the New Testament and the Fathers to Recent Times*, Westminster, Maryland: Newman, 1959.

Gutierrez, Gustavo, *We Drink from Our Own Wells: The Spiritual Journey of a People*, SCM Press, 1984.

Hanson, Bradley, *Christian Spirituality and Spiritual Theology*, Dialogue 21/3 Summer 1982, pages 207–12.

Hanson, Bradley, editor, *Christian Spirituality: Methodological and Historical Essays*, Atlanta: Scholars Press, 1990. (American Academy of Religion Studies in Religion, Number 62)

Hanson, Bradley, *The Call of Silence: Discovering Christian Meditation*, Minneapolis: Augsburg, 1980.

Hinson, E. Glenn, 'The Theory of Spirituality', *One in Christ*, 17/3 1981, pages 244–49.

Hoffman, Bengt R., *Luther and the Mystics: A Re-examination of Luther's Spiritual Experience and His Relation to the Mystics*, Minneapolis: Augsburg, 1976.

Holmes, Urban T., III, *A Brief History of Christian Spirituality*, New York: Seabury, 1981.

Holmes, Urban T., III, *Daily Living in the Twelfth Century*, Greenwood Press, 1994.

Holmes, Urban T., III, *Spirituality for Ministry*, San Francisco: Harper and Row, 1982.

Hosmer, Rachel, 'Current Literature on Spirituality (Review Article)', *Anglican Theological Review* LXVI: 4, pages 423–41.

Hulme, William E., *Let the Spirit In: Practicing Christian Devotional Meditation*, Nashville: Abingdon, 1979.

Ilunga, Bukole, Wa, *Paths of Liberation: A Third World Spirituality*, Maryknoll, New York: Orbis, 1984.

Jantzen, Grace M., *Julian of Norwich: Mystic and Theologian*, SPCK, 1992.

Jodock, Darrell, *The Church's Bible: Its Contemporary Authority*, Minneapolis: Fortress, 1989.

Jones, Cheslyn, Geoffrey Wainwright and Edward Yarnold, editors, *The Study of Spirituality*, SPCK, 1994.

Julian of Norwich, *Revelations of Divine Love*, translated by James Walsh, A. Clarke Books, n.d.

Jungmann, Joseph A., *Christian Prayer through the Centuries*, translated by John Coyne, New York: Paulist Press, 1978.

Kavanaugh, Kieran and Otilio Rodriguez, editors, *The Collected Works of St John of the Cross*, Washington, DC: ICS Publications, Institute of Carmelite Studies, 1979.

Keller, John, *Let Go, Let God*, Minneapolis: Augsburg, 1985

Kempis, Thomas, *The Imitation of Christ*, A. Clarke Books, 1980.

Klug, Ron and Lyn, *Faithful Hearts, Faithful Hands*, Rejoice Curriculum for Adults, Minneapolis: Augsburg, 1992.

Knowles, David, *Christian Monasticism*, New York: McGraw-Hill, 1969.

Knowles, David, *From Pachomius to Ignatius: A Study in the Constitutional History of the Religious Orders*, Oxford University Press, 1966.

Knowles, David, *What is Mysticism?*, Sheed and Ward, 1989.

Koyama, Kosuke, *Three Mile an Hour God*, SCM Press, 1979.

Koyama, Kosuke, *Waterbuffalo Theology*, SCM Press, 1974.

Lawrence, C.H., *Medieval Monasticism*, second edition, New York: Longman, 1989.

Leclercq, Jean, François Vandenbroucke and Louis Bouyer, *The Spirituality of the Middle Ages*, Burns and Oates, 1968. (Volume 2 of *A History of Christian Spirituality*)

Leech, Kenneth, *Soul Friend: Spiritual Direction in the Modern World*, Darton, Longman and Todd, 1994.

Leech, Kenneth, *True Prayer: An Introduction to Christian Spirituality*, Sheldon, 1980.

Luibheid, Colm, translator, *Pseudo-Dionysius: The Complete Works*, New York: Paulist Press, 1987.

Lundin, Roger and Mark A. Noll, *Voices from the Heart: Four Centuries of American Piety*, Grand Rapids, Michigan: Eerdmans, 1987.

Luther, Martin, 'A Simple Way to Pray', *Luther's Works*, Philadelphia: Fortress, 1968, volume 43, pages 187–212.

MacNutt, Francis, *Healing*, Hodder, 1989.

The Life of Madame Guyon, Cambridge: J. Clarke, 1961.

Marshall, Michael, *The Restless Heart: The Life and Influence of St Augustine*, Grand Rapids: Eerdmans, 1987.

McCarty, Doran, 'Southern Baptist Spirituality', *One in Christ*, 17/3 1981, pages 250–54.

McCarty, Doran, 'Spirituality: A Southern Baptist Perspective', *Review and Expositer*, 79/2 Spring 1982, pages 307–11.

McGinn, Bernard and John Meyendorff, editors, *Christian Spirituality: Origins to the Twelfth Century*, SCM Press, n.d. (Volume 16 of World Spirituality)

Merton, Thomas, *The Last of the Fathers: Saint Bernard of Clairvaux and the Encyclical Letter, Doctor Mellifluus*, New York: Harcourt, Brace and Co., 1954.

Merton, Thomas, *The Wisdom of the Desert: Sayings from the Desert Fathers of the Fourth Century*, D. Anderson Books, 1990.

Meyendorff, John, *Byzantine Theology: Historical Trends and Doctrinal Themes*, Fordham University Press, 1993.

Mott, Michael, *The Seven Mountains of Thomas Merton*, Sheldon Press, 1986.

Mulhearn, Timothy, editor, *Getting it All Together: The Heritage of Thomas Merton*, Wilmington, Delaware: Michael Glazier, 1984.

Neal, Marie Augusta, SND, deN, *A Socio-Theology of Letting Go: The Role of a First World Church Facing Third World Peoples*, New York: Paulist Press, 1997.

Nouwen, Henri J.M., *Heart Speaks to Heart: Three Prayers to Jesus*, NotreDame, Indiana: Ave Maria Press, 1989.

Nouwen, Henri J.M., *Making All Things New: An Invitation to the Spiritual Life*, San Francisco: Harper, 1981.

Nouwen, Henri J.M., *Reaching Out: The Three Movements of the Spiritual Life*, Fount, n.d.

Nouwen, Henri J.M., *The Living Reminder: Service and Prayer in Memory of Jesus Christ*, New York: Seabury, 1977.

Nouwen, Henri J.M., *The Way of the Heart: Desert Spirituality and Contemporary Ministry*, New York: Seabury, 1981.

Nouwen, Henri J.M., *The Wounded Healer: Ministry in Contemporary Society*, Darton Longman and Todd, 1994.

O'Donnell, Joseph, 'Spirituality: A Roman Catholic Perspective', *Review and Expositer*, 79/2 Spring 1982, pages 293–305.

O'Donnell, Joseph and Doran McCarty, 'Spirituality: An Epilogue', *Review and Expositer*, 79/2, Spring 1982, pages 312–13.

Ofstedal, Paul, editor, *Daily Readings from Spiritual Classics*, Minneapolis: Augsburg, 1990.

Pelikan, Jaroslav, *Jesus through the Centuries: His Place in the History of Culture*, New Haven: Yale, 1985.

Pelikan, Jaroslav, *The Christian Tradition: A History of the Development of Doctrine*, 5 volumes, Chicago: University of Chicago Press, 1971–89.

Pelikan, Jaroslav, *The Vindication of Tradition*, New Haven: Yale University Press, 1984.

Praying with St Augustine, Triangle, 1987.

Praying with St Teresa of Avila, Triangle, 1988.

Praying with... St Francis of Assisi, Hildegard of Bingen, Catherine of Sienna, Julian of Norwich, etc., Winona, Minnesota: St Mary's Press. (*Companions for the Journey* Series)

Principe, Walter, 'Toward Defining Spirituality', *Studies in Religion*, 12/2 Spring 1983, pages 127–141.

Raitt, Jill, editor, *Christian Spirituality: High Middle Ages and Reformation*, New York:

Crossroad, 1987. (Volume 17 of World Spirituality)

Rakwczy, Susan, IHM, editor, *Common Journey, Different Paths: Spiritual Direction in Cross Cultural Perspective*, Maryknoll, New York: Orbis, 1992.

Roberts, Robert C., 'What is Spirituality?' *Reformed Journal* 33/8 August 1983, pages 14–18.

Sager, Allan H., *Gospel-Centered Spirituality: An Introduction to Our Spiritual Journey*, Minneapolis: Augsburg, 1990.

Schramm, Mary, 'A Wonderful Word: Enough', *Extravagant Love*, Minneapolis: Augsburg, 1988, pages 74–85.

Sellner, Edward C., *Mentoring: The Ministry of Spiritual Kinship*, Notre Dame, Indiana: Ave Maria Press, 1990.

Sellner, Edward C., *Soulmaking: The Telling of a Spiritual Journey*, Twenty-third Publications, 1991.

Sellner, Edward C., *The Wisdom of the Celtic Saints*, Ave Maria Press, 1993.

Senn, Frank C., editor, *Protestant Spiritual Traditions*, New York: Paulist Press, 1986.

Sittler, Joseph A., 'Spirituality and Discipline', *Word and World*, pages 123–28.

Shafer, Ingrid H., *Eros and the Womanliness of God: Andrew Greeley's Romances of Renewal*, Chicago: Loyola University Press, 1986.

Shorter, Aylward, *African Christian Spirituality*, New York: Macmillan, 1978.

Spener, Philip Jacob, *Pia Desideria*, Minneapolis: Fortress, 1989 (1964).

Sponheim, Paul R., editor, *A Primer on Prayer*, Philadelphia: Fortress, 1988.

Steere, Douglas V., editor, *Quaker Spirituality: Selected Writings*, New York: Paulist Press, 1984. (*Classics of Western Spirituality* Series)

Timmerman, John H., *Sexuality and Spiritual Growth*, New York: Crossroad, 1992.

Trobisch, Walter, 'Martin Luther's Quiet Time', *Complete Works of Walter Trobisch*, Downers Grove, Illinois: Intervarsity, 1987, pages 703–14.

Tugwell, Simon, OP, *Ways of Imperfection*, Springfield, Illinois: Templegate, 1985.

Van der Bent, Ans, 'The Concern for Spirituality: An Analytical and Bibliographical Survey of the Discussion within the WCC Constituency', *Ecumenical Review*, 38/1 January 1986, pages 101–14.

Volz, Carl A., *Faith and Practice in the Early Church: Foundations for Contemporary Theology*, Minneapolis: Augsburg, 1983.

Waddell, Helen, *The Desert Fathers*, Constable, 1995.

Wainwright, Geoffrey, 'Christian Spirituality', *The Encyclopedia of Religion*, New York: Macmillan, volume 3, pages 452–60.

Wainwright, Geoffrey, *Doxology: The Praise of God in Worship, Doctrine, and Life*, New York: Oxford University Press, 1980.

Wakefield, Gordon S., editor, *Dictionary of Christian Spirituality*, SCM Press, 1990.

Ward, Benedicta, *The Desert Christian: Sayings of the Desert Fathers: The Alphabetical Collection*, New York: Macmillan, 1980.

Ware, Timothy, editor, *The Art of Prayer: An Orthodox Anthology*, London: Faber, 1966.

Williams, Rowan, *Wound of Knowledge: Christian Spirituality: from the New Testament to St John of the Cross*, Darton, Longman and Todd, 1990.

Index of Names

INDEX OF NAMES

Index of Subjects

Acknowledgments

African prayers are from *An African Prayer Book*, Desmond Tutu (ed.) (New York/London: Doubleday, 1995). Used by permission of Doubleday, a division of Bantam, Doubleday, Dell Publishing Group, Inc.

Excerpts from the Odes of Solomon are from *The Old Testament Pseudepigrapha*, James H. Charlesworth (ed.) (Garden City, NY: Doubleday, 1985). Used by permission of Doubleday, a division of Bantam, Doubleday, Dell Publishing Group, Inc.

Excerpts from Pseudo-Dionysius are from *Pseudo-Dionysius: The Complete Works* (New York: Paulist Press, 1987). Used by permission of Paulist Press, 997 Macarthur Boulevard, Mahwah, NJ 07430.

Excerpts from *The Collected Works of St John of the Cross*, translated by Kieran Kavanagh and Otilio Rodriguez (copyright © 1979 Washington Province of Discalced Carmelites), are used by permission of ICS Publications, 2131 Lincoln Road NE, Washington, DC 20002.

Sample of a celtic poem prayer is from *The Celtic Vision: Prayers and Blessings* from the Outer Hebrides, (Darton, Longman and Todd, 1988). Used by permission of Darton, Longman and Todd, 1 Spencer Court, 140–142 Wandsworth High Street, London SW18 4JJ.

Sayings of the Desert Fathers are from *The Desert Christian: Sayings of the Desert Fathers: The Alphabetical Collection*, (New York: Macmillan, 1980). Used by permission of Paramount Publishing, 1230 Avenue of the Americas, New York, NY 10020.

The Twelve Steps of Alcoholics Anonymous are from *Alcoholics Anonymous*, 3rd edition (New York: AA World Services). Used by permission of Alcoholics Anonymous World Services, Inc. Permission to reprint does not mean that AA has reviewed or approved the contents of this publication, nor that AA agrees with the views expressed herein. AA is a program of recovery from alcoholism—use of the Twelve Steps in connection with programs and activities which are patterned after AA, but which address other problems, does not imply otherwise.